The
Upward
Journey

RUSSELL
LEITCH

THE
UPWARD
JOURNEY

Pleasant W rd
A Division of WINEPRESS PUBLISHING

Pleasant Word (a division of WinePress Publishing, PO Box 428, Enumclaw, WA 98022) functions only as book publisher. As such, the ultimate design, content, editorial accuracy, and views expressed or implied in this work are those of the author.

Unless otherwise noted, all Scriptures are taken from the *King James Version* of the Bible.

ISBN 13: 978-1-4141-0984-8
ISBN 10: 1-4141-0984-9
Library of Congress Catalog Card Number: 2007901764

This work is dedicated to
God my Father, who created me,
to Jesus my Lord, who saved me,
and to the Holy Spirit, who empowered me.

TABLE OF CONTENTS

Acknowledgments

My heartfelt thanks to Nancy, my dear wife of 50 years, who has been patient beyond expectation as I spent countless hours secluded from her to work on this volume.

Thanks to my longstanding friend Bob Greene, whose transcriptions and editing expertise helped immensely through several revisions and whose patience with my stumbling efforts has been exponential.

Thanks to Henry Hosley III, who developed the cover image with his remarkable skill at computer work and his great talent for artistic design.

And thanks to Holy Spirit, our senior editor, who prompted and directed this work to be done. May all the praise, honor, and glory be to Him.

I am aware that this is a product of my best effort. I hope and pray that it will prove of value to the reader in opening a wider realm of thought and consideration of this "so great salvation" that we have been given.

PROLOGUE

It has often been said that it is not sufficient for us just to know the truth; it must be our lifestyle. Many have been deceived into believing that they *are* something because they *know* something. However, knowledge not expressed in life is only information. The religiously informed soul (mind, will, emotion) not under the direction and control of the Holy Spirit is one of the worst dangers facing the Body of Christ (see Romans 8:1-8). Religious knowledge mixed with worldly method or personal opinion does not express wisdom from above but is wisdom that is earthly, sensual and devilish (see James 3:13-17).

It is my hope that this book will help Christians to make the transition from simply knowing the truth to actually living the truth. If we are living the truth, it will be evident because we will be increasing in Christlikeness—becoming like Jesus, who is the truth.

> And we know that all things work together for good to them that love God, to them who are the called according to his purpose. For whom he did foreknow, he also did predestinate to be conformed to the image of his Son, that he might be the firstborn among many brethren.
>
> (Romans 8:28-29)

INTRODUCTION

When we begin a journey, we must know our place of beginning so we can identify the route to our destination. Scripture tells us the starting point common to all:

> For all have sinned, and come short of the glory of God.
>
> (Romans 3:23)

> As it is written, There is none righteous, no, not one: There is none that understandeth, there is none that seeketh after God. They are all gone out of the way, they are together become unprofitable; there is none that doeth good, no, not one.
>
> (Romans 3:10-12)

We will examine the thought, motive and attitude changes that must occur in our lives to bring us to Christlikeness in this life (see Ephesians 4:13).

> I beseech you therefore, brethren, by the mercies of God, that ye present your bodies a living sacrifice, holy, acceptable unto God, which is your reasonable service. And be not conformed to this world: but be ye transformed by the renewing of your mind, that ye may prove what is that good, and acceptable, and perfect, will of God.
>
> (Romans 12:1-2)

The word "renewing" in this passage is from a Greek word meaning a complete reversal from what was to something new that has never before existed. Our journey consists of many small steps involving every aspect of our lives. We may often stumble and occasionally fall. We may not have taken the first step in one area yet be mature in another area. Our lives are a series of progressions and repetitions as we travel along our upward journey toward Christian maturity. God's way is change and more change.

> Brethren, I count not myself to have apprehended: but this one thing I do, forgetting those things which are behind, and reaching forth unto those things which are before, I press toward the mark for the prize of the high calling of God in Christ Jesus.
>
> (Philippians 3:13-14)

> When I was a child, I spake as a child, I understood as a child, I thought as a child: but when I became a man, I put away childish things.
>
> (2 Corinthians 13:11)

> That ye put off concerning the former conversation the old man, which is corrupt according to the deceitful lusts; And be renewed in the spirit of your mind; And that ye put on the new man, which after God is created in righteousness and true holiness.
>
> (Ephesians 4:22-24)

As Christians, we may be at different places in the journey. Yet we should all travel together and respect each other regardless of our individual progress. This is not something we can do in our own strength; only God working in us and through us can accomplish it (see 2 Corinthians 3:18).

And the very God of peace sanctify you wholly; and I pray God your whole spirit and soul and body be preserved blameless unto the coming of our Lord Jesus Christ. Faithful is he that calleth you, who also will do it.

(1 Thessalonians 5:23-24)

The word "do" means to supply the wisdom, energy, and power to accomplish something. God does the work. We experience the change by yielding and cooperating. Being born-again is only the beginning of the Christian life. We must make many changes to progress in maturity and wholeness.

Chapter 1

CONVERSION

Do you think that conversion and being born-again is the same thing?

Christians often use the word "conversion" when they are actually speaking of regeneration or the new birth. I believe this is an error. The words that our Bible translates as "conversion" and "regeneration" are not the same in the Greek, nor do they have similar meanings. When we discuss conversion, we must therefore understand its meaning according to the original language of the New Testament.

The Greek word for "conversion" is *epistrepho,* which means to be turned about, to turn around or to turn toward. It literally means turning around and facing a new direction. This has nothing to do with the Greek word that means "new birth," which is an act of God that occurs by grace. God births us brand-new by His Spirit; however, we turn ourselves around. New birth is His initiative; turning around is our initiative. New birth is an act of God's will; turning around (conversion) is an act of our will.

And in them is fulfilled the prophecy of [Isaiah], which saith, By hearing ye shall hear, and shall not understand; and seeing ye shall see, and shall not perceive: For this people's heart is waxed gross, and their ears are dull of hearing, and their eyes they have closed; lest at any time they should see with their eyes and hear with their ears, and should understand with their heart, and should be converted, and I should heal them.

(Matthew 13:14-15)

Jesus said that the people who had gathered to hear Him had hearts that "waxed gross" (stupefy, render callous) and ears that were dull. The Messiah, the Son of God, stood before them, but they didn't recognize Him. Their hearts had been hardened. They were spiritually blind.

Many Christians today are no different. We can become so wrapped up in ourselves, in our concerns, in the issues of our lives and in our habitual religious practices that we miss the Lord. Shocking but true! Born-again Christians can miss the purpose of God in their lives because they have not turned around and looked in the right direction. They do not behold the King and His kingdom.

Jesus said that He would heal us when we "converted" and turned toward Him. To be healed means to be made whole or to repair thoroughly.

Verily I say unto you, Whosoever shall not receive the kingdom of God as a little child, he shall not enter therein.

(Mark 10:15)

We must become as a little child. By this, Jesus did not mean that we become childish but rather that we become childlike, as in a parent-child relationship. We are God's children, and He is our loving parent. He cares for us because He is our Father. That is our true relationship with God. He said that if we don't become God-dependent, we will not enter the kingdom of God. We must humble ourselves. Humility is emphasized in Scripture because to become as little children, we must leave independence and self-sufficiency behind.

Some of us may have thought that when God saved us, He got a bargain. We believed that we had much to offer God for use in His kingdom. In reality, our perceived strengths are more of a problem to the Lord than our actual weaknesses, because we believe and act as if we can handle things alone. God must get that self-sufficient pride out of us before He can enable us to do what He wants. We need to be converted and turn our perceptions and attitudes around.

> And the Lord said, Simon, Simon, behold, Satan hath desired to have you, that he may sift you as wheat: But I have prayed for thee, that thy faith fail not: and *when thou art converted*, strengthen thy brethren.
>
> (Luke 22:31-32, emphasis added)

Peter declared that he was ready to die with Jesus if it were necessary. Yet when tested, Peter fell into the sin of denying the Lord because he was confused and afraid. Jesus had said this was going to happen. After Peter was again oriented toward the kingdom of God, Jesus told him to strengthen his brethren and encourage them. Peter turned away in his weakness. After he was converted, he turned back in God's strength.

> Repent ye therefore, and be converted, that your sins may be blotted out, when the times of refreshing shall come from the presence of the Lord.
>
> (Acts 3:19)

When we repent, we turn from the old to the new and enter into a time of spiritual refreshing. If we do not truly repent, we will continue committing the same sins. If we don't turn around, we will miss the times of refreshing.

> And being brought on their way by the church, they passed through Phenice and Samaria, declaring the conversion of the Gentiles; and they caused great joy unto all the brethren.
>
> (Acts 15:3)

The Gentiles' conversion was a turning toward God and a turning away from idols. Self is an idol in our lives. We are to turn from being self-centered to being God-centered.

> For they themselves show us what manner of entering in we had unto you, and how ye turned to God from the idols to serve the living and true God.
>
> (1 Thessalonians 1:9)

My wife and I once had a dispute that lasted the better part of the day. We couldn't—or wouldn't—resolve it. After watching the evening news, I went to the kitchen for a snack. As I put my hand on the refrigerator handle, the Lord spoke to me and said, "What are you doing?" I answered, "I am getting that leftover dessert as a snack." The Lord said, "Actually, you are committing idolatry." I recoiled from the refrigerator and asked for understanding. The Lord said, "Instead of coming to Me to resolve the dispute with your wife, you are seeking to make yourself feel better by eating food." I repented immediately, *turned around,* and went to prayer.

Regeneration is different from turning around (conversion); it is a *new* beginning, a *new* birth. It refers specifically to a spiritual rebirth. In biblical times, this particular word denoted the restoration of something to its pristine state—to an uncorrupted, unpolluted, and pure state. It meant bringing something back to its pure beginning. It meant restoration of something that had gone wrong to make it right.

> Not by works of righteousness which we have done, but according to His mercy He saved us, by the washing of regeneration, and renewing of the Holy Ghost.
>
> (Titus 3:5)

The phrase translated "washing of regeneration" comes from the same root word in Greek that translates as "new nativity." The word translated "regeneration" is the Greek word *paliggenesia.* *Palig* means "anew, once more, or again," while *genesia* means "beginning."

> Jesus answered and said unto him, Verily, verily, I say unto thee, Except a man be born-again, he cannot see the kingdom of God.
>
> (John 3:3)

The phrase translated "born-again" is comprised of two Greek words. One is *gennao*, from the root *genesis*, meaning "birth." The second word is *anothen*, which means "again." Sometimes the two words are translated "new birth" and sometimes "born-again."

The word *gennao* can also be translated to be born, to procreate, or to be delivered of. As it relates to *genesis*, or being born, it refers to the birth delivery process. It does not mean to simply repair something—it is a *brand-new birth* process that produces something that never existed before.

The words for regeneration and new birth are related. Thus, we can correctly use the terms "regeneration," "new birth" or "born-again" interchangeably. However, we are not correct when we use the term "conversion" or "converted" to mean born-again.

> But as many as received him, to them gave he power to become the sons of God, even to them that believe on his name: Which were born, not of blood, nor of the will of the flesh, nor of the will of man, but of God.
>
> (John 1:12-13)

The word translated as "power" means the granting of privilege and the authority of relational identity with God. We weren't born-again because we chose to be born-again but because God brought us to a new birth. We became alive in Jesus.

Jesus said, "Except a man be born again, he cannot see the kingdom of God." The word "see" means to perceive or to understand. When the new birth occurs, our spiritual eyes and ears are opened and our hearts are able to perceive the things of the Spirit. God had to make changes in us to enable us to perceive His spiritual realm.

John 3:5 tells us that we must be born of the water and of the Spirit before we can enter the kingdom of God. The word "enter" means to partake fully, to enjoy, to participate, or to be a part of. We do not fully experience the Kingdom unless we go all the way into it. Unfortunately, many born-again Christians see, but never fully enter, the kingdom of God.

Once we are saved, we *see* the kingdom of God. However, we can only *enter* the kingdom of God by the water and by the Spirit. We must pass through a progression of life-changing experiences to come to a place in which we are living, moving, and having our being in Jesus and truly dwelling in His kingdom (see Acts 17:28).

In Mark 2:21-22, Jesus uses the examples of mending old cloth with a new cloth patch and putting new wine into old wineskins. Jesus used knowledge common in His day to help people understand that the old and the new were not compatible.

We must put off the old self-centered person before we can put on the new God-centered person. If we attempt to graft the new person in Jesus onto the old person, we will fall back into the sinful world rather than being renewed and living in the kingdom of God. The new nature we receive with the new birth is not compatible with the pattern of our former life. Our motives and attitudes must change after we come to the Lord through the new birth. We deceive ourselves if we think we can cling to some of that "good stuff" that we had in our old lives and bring it into our new lives in Jesus. We gradually, and willingly, give up even that which we once thought was good.

Genesis 2:7 describes the creation of human life. God made Adam, and then He breathed the breath of life into him. Because our ancestor Adam died (was spiritually separated from God) in his sin, we were born dead in our sin. We have no life in God until the Holy Spirit breaths His life into us, thus giving us a new birth (creation of a new spiritual life).

In John 20:22, Jesus said "receive ye the Holy Ghost" as He breathed on His disciples—an action that is parallel to the Genesis account in which God gave life to Adam by breathing into him the breath of life. The disciples received the person of the Holy

Spirit, who gave them new birth, shortly before Jesus ascended into heaven. They did not receive the baptism of power. That came on Pentecost.

Every person initially is born of Adam's race. We were alive only to things of the spiritual realm in which we were born, which is the kingdom of darkness. This is why many people who are searching for spiritual meaning engage in New Age or occult practices. The enemy deceives them into following the wrong spiritual path to keep them dead and separated from the Spirit of God. The human spirit is not functionally dead, but it is dead in the sense that it has no living connection with God.

Our spirits were born anew with the new birth, but we live in the same body. Our soul (will, mind, and emotions) does not change immediately. Our old self still wants its own way.

In 1 Corinthians 2:12-14, Paul tells us that the natural man cannot perceive the things of God's spirit because they can be discerned only through God's spirit. When our human spirits are regenerated (born-again)—have the life of God breathed into them— our *dead* spirits become *alive* to God. We can then experience the fullness of life by His Spirit.

In 1 Corinthians 6:17, Paul states, "But he that is joined unto the Lord is one spirit." The word "joined" means superglued. Jesus is glued to us, and we are stuck to Him. Our renewed human spirit is joined to His Holy Spirit. It is like marriage, where a man and woman join together to become a new entity (see Genesis 2:24).

In 2 Corinthians 5:17, Paul declares, "Old things are passed away; behold all things are become new." Does this mean that we were completely healed in our physical body the moment we became saved? Does it mean that the demons automatically left us? Does it mean that our nature immediately changed? Of course not! This is a positional truth that states we became brand-new people in the sight of God when we were born-again. Old things passed away (and are still passing away) and all things became new (and are still becoming new). It takes time for this positional truth to work out in our lives. We must grasp it and through prayer and faith make it become experience. We are required to work out our salvation with fear and trembling (see Philippians 2:12). This is a process.

In Ephesians 4:23, Paul says, "Be renewed in the spirit of your mind." The word "renewed" as used here means to have the functions of our minds spiritually transformed. We change from what and how we used to think to completely new processes of thought and reasoning. As Jethro sang to Moses in the animated film *The Prince of Egypt*, "You must see through heaven's eyes."

In 1 Peter 1:23, Peter proclaims, "Being born again, not of corruptible seed, but of incorruptible, by the word of God, which liveth and abideth forever." Peter says that we were born-again by *incorruptible* seed. We received our heavenly Father's spiritual DNA. The Holy Spirit established us in the family of God as the heavenly Father's natural-born children. We must put off the old so we can put on the new (see Zechariah 3:1-4).

> Whosoever believeth that Jesus is the Christ is born of God.
>
> (1 John 5:1)

The word "believeth" means much more than intellectual assent. When someone truly believes, he or she becomes so convinced of something that he or she takes irrevocable action on the basis of that belief. When Peter stepped out of the boat, he believed that Jesus would make the water hold him up. He took action on the basis of his belief. It was irrevocable. The moment Peter saw the wind and the waves and stopped believing he would be upheld on the water, he began to sink. We shouldn't judge Peter too harshly. After all, he was the only one of the disciples to get out of the boat. Too many Christians today are afraid to *get out of the boat.*

In 1 John 5:4, we are told, "That which is born of God overcomes the world." In other words, that which is born of God is godly in its completion but not necessarily in its initiation. We overcome the world not because *we* overcome it but because *Jesus* overcame it for us (see John 16:33). As we become like Him, we overcome. To the degree that we are not conformed to Jesus, we have not yet overcome.

> We know that whosoever is born of God sinneth not; but he
> that is begotten of God keepeth himself, and that wicked one
> toucheth him not.
>
> (1 John 5:18)

Whoever is born of God does not sin willfully and habitually. Do we have a way to go? Yes, we do! Have we made some progress already? Yes, we have! In some instances, we can look sin—that which used to overcome us— in the face and say, "*no!*" and then walk past the temptation. We have overcome some of our Adam nature. We are destined to overcome all of it.

Repentance is a specific, continuous, and essential choice of our new nature. It is not repentance at the point of salvation only; it is repentance on a continuing basis. In Romans 2:4, Paul writes, "The goodness of God leadeth thee to repentance." It is God's love that convinces us to change our minds. When we change our minds, we turn away from the old and turn toward the new.

Scripture records some dramatic conversions. In 1 Kings 19, God instructed Elijah to anoint Elisha to be a prophet, so Elijah cast his mantle, the symbol of his prophetic authority, upon Elisha. Once the mantle had been passed, Elisha said goodbye to his family and butchered the oxen with which he had been plowing the fields. He placed the very valuable yoke, bars and harnesses into a pile and burned them as an offering to God. He blessed his family with a feast of the oxen.

Elisha made such a conversion (full turn around) that he couldn't go back to farming because he no longer had the oxen, harness, or farm implements. His goodbye to his family was symbolic of the release of the security of worldly relationships. The evidence of his conversion was his turning around to face in another direction and completely leaving what was behind.

Jesus cast His mantle upon us when He ascended into heaven. He said, "The works that I do, shall he do also"(John 14:12). By doing so, Jesus conferred His authority upon us. We are now to be *in* the world but not *of* the world (see John 17:15-16). This marked the end of our being governed by worldly relationships.

We are to now walk a different path and are expected to submit to the will of God and live His ways.

Paul exhorts us to forget the things that are behind and respond to the higher calling in Jesus (see Philippians 3:13). It is a call to let go of worldly activities that would hinder us as we follow the Lord.

Mark 1:16-20 records the calling of Simon, Andrew, James, and John. Each of these men instantly followed Jesus at once and without delay. They didn't make excuses. They simply *turned away* from what they were doing, *turned to* Jesus and followed Him.

In Mark 2:13-14, we read about the calling of Matthew. He was sitting at his table collecting taxes, probably making more than a good living, when Jesus walked up to him and said, "Follow me." Matthew *immediately walked away* from the graft and corruption and the riches of the world. He left his high-income position, which he had probably bought at great expense, and followed Jesus. He left everything behind.

In Acts 16:9, Paul describes a heavenly vision in which a man from Macedonia beckoned Paul, saying, "Come over into Macedonia and help us." Paul immediately endeavored to comply, which means he made a strong effort to go promptly to Macedonia in answer to God's calling. In the same way, we may be called of God from one work to go to another work. If we continue in what God has called us to stop doing, we will be clinging on to something that has no life. We are born-again once but may experience many conversions as we follow the Lord.

> What? Know ye not that your body is the temple of the Holy Ghost which is in you, which ye have of God, and ye are not your own? For ye are bought with a price: therefore glorify God in your body, and in your spirit, which are God's.
>
> (1 Corinthians 6:19-20)

When we became Christians, we opened our lives and invited Jesus to come in and be part of us. Yet He has no interest in merely being *part* of us—He wants *all* of our person to become like Him. We don't always see it like that at first, but we slowly learn. Jesus doesn't want to be added to our lives; He wants to consume our lives until only His life remains. We do not own this new life—it belongs to Jesus. Many Christians never reach spiritual maturity because they do not fully convert.

Before we experienced the new birth, we focused on and interacted with the entire world and its ways, systems, and activities. However, the instant we were born-again, a line of division was drawn, as it were, right across our toes. This is the boundary between darkness and light, between the family of the world and the family of God. We are now *in* the world but not *of* the world. We may still face the world and remain focused on all the world has to offer us. However, since we are and become what we behold, our life expression will remain essentially worldly until we turn around fully (convert) and make God's kingdom our primary focus.

So what is it that we are beholding, or earnestly focused on? Have we really, entirely, put the world behind us? Or are we maybe only "half-turned"? Many people are born-again, but they have not converted. The world still intrigues them. They do not grow spiritually, because they have not turned their backs on the attractions of the world that distract them from Jesus. They will not enjoy the quality of eternal life while on earth because they do not see it. They are looking in the wrong direction.

After we are born-again and converted, we are still in such close proximity to the kingdom of darkness that the fiery arrows of the "raiding parties" of the enemy can easily reach us. We must separate ourselves by moving further into the kingdom of God (light) and leave worldly attitudes and ungodly activities (darkness) well behind us.

Chapter 2

SEPARATION

Have you disconnected yourself from those people or activities that will hinder your walk with the Lord? Or are you still hanging on to the comfortable and familiar even if you know they are not beneficial? If God has not assigned you to that place, why are you there?

> And what agreement hath the temple of God with idols? For ye are the temple of the living God; as God hath said, I will dwell in [them], and walk in them; and I will be their God, and they shall be my people. Wherefore come out from among them, and be ye separate, saith the Lord, and touch not the unclean [thing]; and I will receive you, And will be a Father unto you, and ye shall be my sons and daughters, saith the Lord Almighty.
>
> (2 Corinthians 6:16-18)

The word "separate" means to divide between, establish a boundary, distinguish one from another or see something as recognizably different. We may turn around (be converted) and look in another direction (toward the Kingdom) but remain stationary, never separating from our old lives. Separation means we have changed our associations and behavior. Christians must separate from five things:

29

- First, we must separate from things that are spiritually unclean, such as inanimate objects that are defiled.
- Second, we must separate from spiritually unclean people. We should not have fellowship with those who are involved in occult practices, spiritualism, witchcraft and so forth, except in a righteous and redemptive way.
- Third, we must separate ourselves from the unclean actions, words, and deeds of others. If we are associating with people who are doing wrong things, God wants us to simply say goodbye and then turn around and walk away.
- Fourth, we must separate from false believers. False believers are not false because they directly serve Satan but because they serve self. We must separate from those who call themselves Christians but who are bearing bad fruit and refuse to change. A person's mistake is not the basis for separation—the basis for separation is the refusal to change. Churches that split over minor doctrinal differences or personal disputes wound the Lord.
- Fifth, we must separate from people who are like those described in 2 Timothy 3:5 as "having a form of godliness, but deny the power thereof."

SEPARATION FROM UNCLEAN THINGS

Deuteronomy 7:26 says, "Neither shall thou bring an abomination into thine house, lest thou be a cursed thing like it: but thou shalt utterly detest it, and thou shalt utterly abhor it; for it [is] a cursed thing." We can bring accursed (spiritually unclean) objects into our homes, which bring defilement. This could be a representation of false religions such as statues of Buddha, Aztec sundials, or African masks. Ask the Lord if you have unclean objects in your home. He will be faithful to show you. He may tell you to destroy an object or merely throw it away.

The book of Numbers tells the story of Korah, who rebelled against Moses. Korah was an unrighteous man. He sought to grasp leadership and priesthood positions even though God had not given them to him. The word of the Lord came to Moses about the judgment that was to come to Korah. The Lord warned the people of Israel to depart (separate) from Korah and his followers and not touch anything that belonged to them. "Depart, I pray you, from the tents of these wicked men, and touch nothing of theirs, lest ye be consumed in all their sins" (Numbers 16:26). The judgment of God was against Korah and everything he owned. If other people touched his possessions, that judgment was to also come on them. Then, by the judgment of God, the earth opened up. Korah, his family and his belongings went into the chasm, and the earth closed over them.

In Joshua 6:17-19, God tells Joshua to keep himself from the "accursed thing." Before the battle of Jericho, God told the Israelites to take no spoils and destroy everything with fire. The Lord claimed the gold and silver, which was consecrated to Him. However, in disobedience to the word of the Lord, Achan took a high priest's robe of the idolatrous religion of Jericho, a wedge of gold and some silver and hid these spoils in his tent. The Israelites lost the next battle. When they prayed and asked God why they lost, God replied that there was sin in the camp. The sin was Achan bringing the accursed spoils into the camp. The entire camp of Israel was cursed because Achan had disobeyed the Lord.

Art objects from other religions can be spiritually unclean, as can ordinary objects that are innocently purchased. In fact, a curse can be placed on an object that brings the curse to a future owner. On more than one occasion, my wife and I have found that the spiritual peace in our home was disturbed after we made a purchase. When we asked the Lord to show us the problem and give us understanding as to why our peace was being disturbed, He would direct our attention to the recently purchased item, which was often manufactured in a non-Christian nation. After we prayed over the purchase, consecrated it to the Lord, broke any idolatrous dedications and drove away any unclean spirits associated with it, the sense of troubling would depart. We need to be wise and not neglect the ways of the Word.

SEPARATION FROM UNCLEAN PEOPLE

Jesus declares in John 17:14-16 that we are *in* the world but not *of* the world. He doesn't mean we should isolate ourselves like hermits or avoid working in a place where there are unsaved people. He doesn't want us physically out of the world, because if we are out of the world, we cannot be witnesses to the world. He wants us to witness to the world but not be part of the world in the sense of agreeing with or participating in the sins of ungodly people. We must distance (separate) ourselves from evil.

In 2 Corinthians 6:14-15, Paul states that we are not to be unequally yoked to an unbeliever. Being "yoked" means to be in a covenant relationship. Our God is a covenant-making God, and the Israelites considered themselves to be His covenant people. They had a special relationship with the Lord. God set the terms of the covenant and what He expected from them.

An unequal yoke means that a believing Christian should not consider marrying a non-Christian. Marriage is a covenant relationship, and God does not want His people marrying unbelievers. If God has chosen a spouse for someone who is not a believer, He will save that person and bring him or her into covenant with Him. The believer is to honor God and do his or her part: pray for that person and wait. If that individual is not the spouse God has chosen, the believer must be willing to let that person go.

My wife and I have seen several instances in which Christians have ignored the directive of the Scripture not to marry an unbeliever. Each time, the Christian said they would lead the person to the Lord after marriage. However, in every case, the unsaved worldly person drew the Christian back into the world. Why? The Christian had disobeyed God and given the enemy opportunity to deceive.

In Ezra 4:3, we read about the Israelites rebuilding the Temple. Jews, Gentiles and some Jews who had married non-Jews wanted to participate. Ezra told those who had married outside the covenant and those who were not Jews that they could not participate in the rebuilding. He recognized that the covenant relationship with God separated the Jews from other nationalities. Those who were not in covenant with God could not help rebuild the Temple.

Ezra called on the Jews who were working on restoring the Temple to be separated from filthiness (see Ezra 6:21). The word "filthiness" in the Bible is most often used to denote religious impurity. In this case, the people were going to the synagogue on the Sabbath and worshiping the Lord, but the remainder of the week they were worshiping a statue of Baal in their home. Ezra told them to end this religious impurity, this spiritual filthiness.

Nehemiah returned to Jerusalem around the same time as Ezra. He had the divine assignment to rebuild the city walls. Nehemiah told the people who were working on the walls to separate themselves from the strangers (meaning people not of Israel). In this instance, God commanded those who were married to non-Jews to end their marriages and send them away. God was not approving of divorce as a general principle but bringing His people back to their covenant relationship. He was calling them back from unclean relationships, back to truth and purity. He was preserving the Holy Seed that would lead to the birth of the Christ. Nehemiah 10:30 records this act of separation.

In Exodus 23:32-33, God commanded Moses to make no covenant with the people of Canaan lest they lead the Jews to sin. God reminded the Israelites that they were not to make any covenant with the people of the land "lest it be for a snare in the midst of thee," that is, a trap, an entanglement or something that would hinder them (see Exodus 34:12).

The book of Joshua relates the story of how a group of Gibeonites came to Joshua and claimed they had come a great distance to meet the Israelites. To make their claim more convincing, they carried moldy bread and dried-out wineskins, rode on dusty camels and wore dirty clothes. The Gibeonites said they had heard about the Israelites' God and what He had done to Og and Sihon of the Amorites. They told Joshua they didn't want any trouble with the Jews and asked him to make a covenant and peace treaty with them. The leaders of Israel, including Joshua, "asked not counsel at the mouth of the LORD" (Joshua 9:14).

Joshua and the leaders of Israel relied on their natural senses. They looked at the moldy bread and all the other apparent evidence and concluded that the Gibeonites must have traveled a long distance. Actually, the Gibeonites lived only three days' journey away. The Israelites were deceived into making a covenant with them, which was contrary to the directive of the Lord. The Gibeonites became a thorn in the side of Israel for all their days, because God required Israel to honor that covenant.

> Whosoever transgresseth, and abideth not in the doctrine of Christ, hath not God. He that abideth in the doctrine of Christ, he hath both the Father and the Son. If there come any unto you, and bring not this doctrine, receive him not into your house, neither bid him God speed: For he that biddeth him God speed is partaker of his evil deeds.
>
> (2 John 9-11)

Members of some cults ring people's doorbells and claim they are making a Christian visit. However, these individuals preach a different Jesus and a different gospel. The Word of God states that we are not to let them into our homes. We are not to welcome them or wish them well in any way. If we do, God warns that He will consider us partakers of their sin. He who agrees with sin is deemed guilty of that sin.

A friend lived with us for a few weeks while he was seeking employment and a permanent place to live. One day, he was at our home alone while we were on a ministry trip when some of these cultists rang the doorbell in their usual style. Our friend, not being aware of this warning in Scripture, invited them in and talked with them at length. He was not well versed enough in Scripture to answer the kind of manipulative spiel that they gave, so he suggested that they should come back when we were home.

When we returned, we immediately sensed a spiritual disturbance and uncleanness in our home. We didn't know why, so we asked our friend, "What happened here while we were gone? This place is unclean. There is a spiritual defilement here." When our friend explained that he had invited two members of this cult into our house, I said, "Well, that explains it." We prayed through until spiritual purity was restored. We learned a lesson that day: God means it when He says not to bring these types of people into our house. If you have done so, repent and pray through your home that it will be cleansed. Discard any literature that these cultists may have left behind.

SEPARATION FROM THE UNCLEAN ACTS OF OTHERS

Scripture admonishes us to separate from the unclean acts of self and others. First, we will deal with the unclean acts of others.

In Acts 2:40, the believers were strongly directed to "save [themselves] from this untoward generation." The word "untoward" means warped, twisted, and perverse. Saving ourselves means we must decide to walk away from the situations and people that would cause us to sin.

Ephesians 5:11 gives another requirement. Paul writes, "Have no fellowship with the unfruitful works of darkness." No means *no!* It doesn't mean partially; it doesn't mean intermittently; it doesn't mean when it is convenient to do so. It means *no fellowship.* We have nothing in common with the works of darkness. We are children of the light.

> Be not deceived: evil communications corrupt good manners.
>
> (1 Corinthians 15:33)

"Communications" in this verse refers to companionship and personal involvement with another. According to *Vine's Expository Dictionary*, "manners" means ethical conduct or morals. If we frequently associate with evil people, we will eventually adapt to their ways and will appear to be no different from them. We are warned that evil companionship corrupts and defiles good morals. Our godly morals and attitudes are to be kept pure from the defilement of this world.

> Depart from me, ye evildoers: for I will keep the command-
> ments of my God.
>
> (Psalms 119:115)

This verse in Psalms suggests that we must be far enough apart from the world so other people can see that we are not associated with evildoers. If we are frequently found in the company of those who act in an ungodly manner, we become associated with them in the eyes and minds of others.

> Abstain from all appearance of evil.
>
> (1 Thessalonians 5:22)

By this, Paul means we must not behave in any way that could even give the appearance that we are sinning, such as a close involvement or relationship with an unrelated person of the opposite sex. No matter how innocent the relationship may be, it gives opportunity for accusation. In Romans 12:9, Paul tells us, "Abhor that which is evil; [consider it disgusting] cleave to that which is good." Make a righteous decision! Turn away! Walk away! Separate yourself! Establish a clear boundary and stay on the righteous side of that boundary.

SEPARATION FROM UNCLEAN ACTS OF SELF

The act of separating ourselves from unclean acts of self raises questions: How do we leave ourselves behind? Are we somehow able separable from ourselves? I believe the Lord shows us that we are. We choose many times each day whether we will allow self to direct our lives or whether we will be directed by the Spirit. *Each choice is a test as to which way of life we will choose.* Are we going to please God, or are we going to please self? Shall we choose to honor and acknowledge God, or shall we submit to the demands of our lower nature?

In Ephesians 4:29 and Colossians 3:8, Paul tells us that we can have corrupt communications. Corrupt communication means that our words spoken from wrong attitudes or a wrong spirit can demean, degrade, or defile others.

Not that which goeth into the mouth defileth a man; but that
which cometh out of the mouth, this defileth a man.

(Matthew 15:11)

Men, if we leaf through a pornographic magazine at a convenience store, we defile ourselves, even if we don't buy it. We
allow defilement and uncleanness to come through our eye-gates
and into our soul where it produces corruption. Of course, we
can't walk around with our eyes closed, so we will see things that
we ought not to gaze at. It might be a scantily dressed female,
suggestive advertising, or something that just jumps up in front
of us. When this occurs, the Word of God instructs us to look
away. We are literally to *turn away.*

I knew a Christian man who owned a donut shop located near
a municipal tennis court. On occasion, some of the women would
come in wearing revealing tennis clothes. They were worldly
people who thought nothing about this. This saint of God kept
an empty donut box on top of the display case. When a scantily
dressed woman came in, he would open the donut box and say,
"Yes ma'am, may I help you?" The top of the donut box shielded
his eyes from the temptation the enemy could use against him.
By acting righteously in this non-aggressive and non-judgmental
way, he honored the will of God.

We can defile ourselves. Deuteronomy 12:30 tells us not to
inquire after the gods of others. The word "inquire" means to
tread, frequent, follow, seek, or ask. If we are born-again Christians on a trip to a foreign country, we should not enter the
temples or shrines of other religions. These places are tainted
with idolatry, given to worship of false gods, and inhabited by
demons. We must exercise wisdom and stay out of these places.
We must not be foolish!

A woman in one of our home groups was interested in ar-
cheology, so she saved up her money and traveled to Egypt. The
ancient objects that she saw there fascinated her. At one point,
her tour group visited a pyramid. They walked up a long ramp
leading to a burial chamber that contained a huge carved stone
sarcophagus. The woman later told us that she felt unsettled when

she entered this chamber. The members of her tour group began acting strange. They gathered together around the sarcophagus in a large circle, held hands and began chanting, "Ommmmm… ommmmm…ommmmm."

Unbeknownst to her, this woman had connected with a group of spiritualists. She hadn't asked God which group she should travel with. She moved to a far corner and prayed in the Spirit. When she did so, the spiritual atmosphere in the room suddenly changed. The people who were chanting around the sarcophagus stopped and moved on.

SEPARATION FROM FALSE BELIEVERS

We must separate from false believers. "False believers" are those people whose lives do not show true repentance. Their lifestyle, behavior, morals, attitudes, and integrity are worldly and unrighteous.

We are admonished in 1 Timothy 5:22 not to be partakers of another person's sin. People may say they are Christians or might actually born-again, but this doesn't mean we can go along with them and do everything they do. We must be wise in the ways of God. We must look at people's lifestyles to see whether or not they are godly. We are not to judge others, but we are to be inspectors of whether they exhibit the fruits of the Spirit.

The word of the Lord once came to the leader of a small group my wife and I attended. The Lord instructed him to relinquish leadership and told him that my wife and I were to lead the meeting for a time. Seven other people in the group confirmed the word. At the time, the man did not perceive the reason. He had fallen into error and had a fleshly attitude. He had begun to produce something out of his own desire rather than what God wanted and had strayed off course. The Lord wanted us to be in the place of leadership not to demean this man but to bring the group back on course.

Unfortunately, this man refused to do what the Lord had clearly told him to do. He rationalized, saying he didn't want to give up leadership of the group and that he must not have heard correctly. The Lord allowed this situation to continue for a short while. Then He brought the issue up again in two different ways: first, with a revelation to a woman through the Word; and second, with a prophetic word. Yet the man still refused to let the Lord have His headship over that meeting and demanded his own way. The next time we were getting ready to attend that meeting, the Lord said, "Stop! You're not going there any more. You will not be a partaker of another man's sin. You are to separate yourselves from him."

We are told in 2 Thessalonians 3:6 to withdraw from a disorderly brother. The word "disorderly" in this verse specifically refers to moral irregularity. For example, if a brother in the Lord frequently goes out with a married woman in the absence of her husband, that brother is disorderly. The leadership of his church needs to admonish and correct him. If he will not receive correction, they must disassociate from him. Isolating him protects other believers. The Holy Spirit will convict him (see John 16:8). Likewise, if an unmarried Christian woman socializes with her married boss, her actions have enough moral irregularity to be questioned and challenged. She shouldn't behave that way. It is wrong.

We are instructed in 2 Thessalonians 3:14-15 to have no company with the disobedient. This doesn't mean that we are to treat disobedient believers (those who willfully disobey the Word of God) as enemies, but simply that we are to have no company with them. We should do what the Word says, not adding or subtracting anything (see Deuteronomy 4:2). Having no company means that we do not have fellowship with these individuals. We do not associate or share meals with them. We simply keep our distance. When we obediently withdraw from someone, the Holy Spirit will convict that person of sin and correct him or her. Note that we are talking about misbehaving believers here. With respect to people of the world (unbelievers), we may have to be where they are, but we don't have to do, or agree with, what they do.

We are warned in 1 Corinthians 5:9-13 not to associate with someone who claims to be a believer but continues in gross sin and refuses to repent. We must expel such a person. This removes the individual from the protective covering of the church and sets him or her apart as being one under discipline. Paul says that we are to "deliver such an one unto Satan for the destruction of the flesh, that the spirit may be saved in the day of the Lord Jesus" (1 Corinthians 5:5). The word "destruction" in this verse does not necessarily mean death or a total loss, but rather conveys the idea of ruin. Paul was saying we must withdraw our protection and prayers. Let Satan get at the person. When that individual gets into enough trouble, he or she will repent. According to 2 Corinthians 2:5-8, this same situation happened in the Corinthian church: A man got into so much trouble when Satan had access through the sin in his life that he repented and was restored to fellowship.

> Now I beseech you, brethren, mark them which cause divisions and offences contrary to the doctrine which ye have learned; and avoid them.
>
> (Romans 16:17)

Vine's Expository Dictionary says that "avoid" means to turn away from those who cause offenses and occasion of stumbling. If we have a brother or sister in the Lord who is walking in falseness (hypocrisy), we are instructed by God to withdraw from him or her. *God holds us accountable to obey His Word.*

We are also told in 1 Timothy 6:4-5 and 11 to withdraw from the contentious and from those who are lovers of money. Some Christians have an inordinate love for money and practice idolatry in the worship of mammon. The Word says we can't serve both God and mammon. We will come to love one and hate the other (see Luke 16:13). God didn't say that it is difficult; He said that we can't. It is not possible.

Contentious people are constantly bickering, finding fault, or starting arguments. We must separate from them and not listen to them. If we do not disconnect from them, we will likely begin to bicker, find fault, and fall into arguments. As Paul wrote, "Know ye not that a little leaven leaveneth the whole lump?" (1 Corinthians 5:6).

We are told in 2 Timothy 3:5 that there are some people who "[have] a form of godliness, but [deny] the power thereof." We must stay away from these people as well. Their error could undermine our faith, which has come to us as a gift from God through our personal experience of the power of the Holy Spirit.

Matthew 18:17 states that we are to separate ourselves from those who will not receive correction. Those who refuse to receive righteous correction are clearly wrong. If the scriptural procedure has been used for correction and they will not receive it, we are to treat them as heathen and publicans (tax collectors). As Christians, how are we supposed to treat heathens and publicans? We pray for them and witness to them, but we do not participate in their sin or have fellowship with them. They are not to partake of the Lord's Supper. We should encourage them to turn to God and treat them as if they are lost—for in a sense, they are. They have not necessarily lost their salvation, but they have lost their way. We must go out of our way to stay out of their way.

I knew of a situation in which a covetous man wanted the pastor's position. The man's wife was very judgmental and critical because of her self-righteousness. The couple became involved in a recreational activity and drew a number of church members into that activity. Through that association, the leaven of self-righteousness, criticism and covetousness began to spread from the couple to several other couples. In the end, it nearly divided the church. How did this happen? The church members, by joining in the activity, didn't avoid the ones who caused division. They didn't obey the Word of God. They gave the enemy opportunity.

> These six [things] doth the LORD hate: yea, seven [are] an abomination unto him: A proud look, a lying tongue, and hands that shed innocent blood, An heart that deviseth wicked imaginations, feet that be swift in running to mischief, A false witness [that] speaketh lies, and he that soweth discord among brethren.
>
> (Proverbs 6:16-19)

If we refuse to obey the Word of the Lord concerning separation, we will bring certain consequences on ourselves. We may have a continuing relationship with God, but we will not have genuine fellowship with Him. Our sin of disobedience separates us from God. Without being separated from wrongdoers, we may still be united to Jesus in Calvary through salvation, but the sin will diminish our intimate, personal relationship with Him. Isaiah wrote:

> Behold, the Lord's hand is not shortened, that it cannot save; neither his ear heavy, that it cannot hear: *But your iniquities have separated between you and your God*, and your sins have hid [his] face from you, that he will not hear.
> (59:1-2, emphasis added)

If we do not separate as the Word requires, the sin of our disobedience will give our enemy opportunity to afflict us. God says that those who walk in the light have fellowship with Him and that those who walk in darkness do not (see 1 John 1:6-7). Those who walk in darkness will have influence without power. They will have activity without achievement. They will have the promise of an abundant life, but they won't have the fulfillment of that promise. We will have the fulfillment of all that God is and says and all of His promises only when we obey Him. The obedience required of all Christians is to separate from unclean objects, unclean people, unclean acts and false brethren. This is the Word of the Lord, and we had better pay attention.

I once had a significant personal experience with the act of separation. I was associated with a Christian leader who exhibited great personality, or soul power. When I was with this person, I could feel the power of his soul pressing on me, expecting or demanding conformance to his ways or his ideas. I knew that this was not the Lord's way, but I didn't know what to do about it.

So I prayed and waited for the Lord to give me wisdom. One day during a meeting with this person, a prayer from the Holy Spirit welled up within me. In my heart I prayed strongly but silently, "Lord, I will fellowship with all of this man's righteousness but none of his unrighteousness." The pressure of his soul power toward me immediately stopped and never resumed despite the many subsequent meetings I had with him. That was a righteous spiritual separation.

As we disconnect ourselves from the powers and ways of the world system, we will begin to experience the power of God's kingdom working in us, for us, and through us.

Chapter 3

POWER

Is it possible for you to do the works of Jesus without the power of Jesus? Is your life and ministry a demonstration of the Spirit and power, or is it just you working hard?

We receive God's power through grace, and it is released through submission. This is not human or soul power. Shortly before His ascension, Jesus instructed His disciples and emphasized what was most important. He said:

> And, behold, I send the promise of my Father upon you; but tarry ye in the city of Jerusalem, until ye be endued with power from on high.
>
> (Luke 24:49)

"Tarry" in this context means to wait, put in right order or let first things come first. "Endued" means to be arrayed with, clothed with, or immersed. God promised that Jesus' followers would receive supernatural power (*dunamis*) and that Jesus would send this power after He ascended to heaven. This is power from on high, which emanates from God, not power of the natural realm, which emanates from other sources. God knows we need His power to enable us to accomplish His perfect will.

> But ye shall receive power, after that the Holy Ghost is come upon you; and ye shall be witnesses unto me both in

> Jerusalem, and in all Judea, and in Samaria, and unto the ut-
> termost part of the earth.
>
> (Acts 1:8)

Dunamis is the root of the word "dynamite." It is Holy Spirit power. A "witness" is one who has seen, heard or felt something and therefore can give a first-hand account of it. Imagine witnessing for Jesus without having seen, felt, or heard Him. At best, we would be explaining a theory, so our witness would be limited. However, if we have experienced God's power and speak of Jesus with that power, our words will carry that power and will be effective.

Although many well-meaning Christians throughout the world have a genuine and zealous love for God, they witness for Jesus without this dynamite power. I am not criticizing them, but how much more could they accomplish if they operated in God's power rather than in their own strength?

> To an inheritance incorruptible, and undefiled, and that
> fadeth not away, reserved in heaven for you, Who are kept
> by the power of God through faith unto salvation ready to be
> revealed in the last time.
>
> (1 Peter 1:4-5)

The word "kept" in this verse means to mount a guard, to protect, to be a watcher in advance, or to put a sentinel on the wall. The phrase "by the power" implies a sense of preparation as well as protection. God watches over us and surrounds us with His presence to keep us safe in the midst of the destructive operations of the Devil.

We often give our enemy too much credit. It is important to remember that God limits Satan's activities (see Job 1:5-12). We will have problems with the world, the flesh and the Devil, but the ultimate power and control belong to God. Jack Deere likes to say, "Trials are the normal lifestyle of maturing Christians."

Faith is a decision to trust God in all things. This trust doesn't come from human intellect. We are to have no confidence in the flesh (natural abilities apart from the Holy Spirit as described in Philippians 3:3) but are to know our God intimately and be confident of His faithfulness, love and power.

> But the people that do know their God shall be strong, and do exploits.
>
> (Daniel 11:32)

> According as his divine power hath given unto us all things that [pertain] unto life and godliness, through the knowledge of him that hath called us to glory and virtue.
>
> (2 Peter 1:3)

"Knowledge" as described in 2 Peter 1:3 does not mean human intellect. It is not reasoning, learning, or human wisdom. It is revelation from the Holy Spirit that is taught, not caught. It is knowledge of Jesus that is personal and experiential. Human reasoning and learning are not bad in themselves, but they cannot be the foundation of our lives.

Vine's Expository Dictionary points out that in Mark 5:28-30, the word "virtue" is the Greek word *dunamis*, which refers to supernatural power. We see evidence of this when God's power is released and miracles occur. Jesus said that He felt virtue (life, power) go out from Him when the woman with the issue of blood touched His robe. When we minister to others in God's power, we may also feel life force (power) go from us and into them.

> Then he answered and spake unto me, saying, This [is] the word of the Lord unto Zerubbabel, saying, Not by might, nor by power, but by my spirit, saith the Lord of hosts. Who [art] thou, O great mountain? Before Zerubbabel [thou shalt become] a plain: and he shall bring forth the headstone [thereof with] shoutings, [crying,] Grace, grace unto it.
>
> (Zechariah 4:6-7)

The Hebrew words for "might" and "power" in this passage refer to human strength and ability. God says we are not to rely on our own strength and ability but on His spirit. When we do, the mountain shall be removed. The word "mountain" in this verse is allegorical for an obstacle to Christian progression (see Matthew 21:21).

> The Lord saveth not with sword and spear: for the battle is the Lord's, and he will give you into our hands.
>
> (1 Samuel 17:47)

God is not limited to the implements of human warfare. We are saved, healed, and delivered by His Word, His grace and His power. What happens when we base our faith on human wisdom? It fails the first time it is tested, because it is sustained by human power. However, if we base our faith on God's divine power and His faithfulness, there are no limits to what can be accomplished.

> And my speech and my preaching [was] not with enticing words of man's wisdom, but in demonstration of the Spirit and of power.
>
> (1 Corinthians 2:4)

Paul's original name was Saul of Tarsus. He studied under Gamaliel, one of the leading rabbis of his time. Paul was one of the most learned of men and was zealous among the Pharisees. He declared, "I am a Pharisee, the son of a Pharisee" (Acts 23:6). When Paul told the Corinthians that he did not use the enticing words of man's wisdom, he did not mean that his learning was worthless but that it wasn't sufficient. He was saying that he came in the demonstration (visible evidence) of the Holy Spirit and power. When the Corinthians saw miracles and signs done by the power of the Spirit, they knew that God was with Paul. God's power confirmed what Paul preached.

> That he would grant you, according to the riches of his glory, to be strengthened with might by his Spirit in the inner man.
>
> (Ephesians 3:16)

Our human spirit is that breath of life we received from God when He created us. Our spirit is often referred to as our "inner man." Our soul and our body comprise our outer being. The Spirit of God empowers the human spirit so that we can rule over our soul (will, mind, and emotions). When the Spirit governs us, we have power and authority over self.

> Now unto him that is able to do exceeding abundantly above all that we ask or think, according to the power that worketh in us.
>
> (Ephesians 3:20)

God can exceed *all* that we ask. His ways are incredibly high above our ways, as the heavens are higher than the earth (see Isaiah 55:9). He puts His Spirit and power within us so that we can be more like Him, increase in intimacy with Him, and do *His* work.

> And what [is] the exceeding greatness of his power to us-ward who believe, according to the working of his mighty power.
>
> (Ephesians 1:19)

Paul could not find words adequate enough to describe the power of God, the exceeding greatness of His power, and the overwhelming strength and surpassing magnitude of that power. Colossal is miniscule compared to this divine power. J. B. Phillip's translation of Ephesians 1:19 reads, "And how tremendous is the power available to us who believe in God."

God invests His power in Christians to further His objective of expanding His kingdom. God intends His power to work through us to help others. God works through us not only to give us blessings but to also, more importantly, accomplish His Kingdom purposes. God's power heals us, delivers us, saves us, frees us from sin, and gives us instruction and direction. God intends that power to work through us and influence the lives of others.

> And he said, Thy name shall be called no more Jacob, but Israel: for as a prince hast thou power with God and with men, and has prevailed.
>
> (Genesis 32:28)

The word "Israel" is comprised of two words in the original Hebrew: *Yisra* and *El*. *El* means God. Some scholars believe that *Yisra* is *not* rooted in the word translated as contender or strength but rather in the word that means to rule. Thus, they believe that rather than Israel meaning one who has struggled or wrestled with God, the meaning of the word is one who is ruled by God. The implications are quite different, because if God is ruling us, we are governed and led by the Holy Spirit. I believe in my heart—although I could be wrong—that Israel means God rules.

> I can do all things through Christ which strengtheneth me.
>
> (Philippians 4:13)

We cannot do what *we* want. We are enabled (empowered) to do everything that God wants. My wife and I were given a small card with the most beautiful yet simple statement: *The will of God will never lead you where the grace of God cannot keep you.* God's power enables us to go where He sends us and do what He wants done.

We are never given license to use God's power for selfish purposes. If we are ruled and led by the Spirit, the Spirit will produce works that glorify God. If the flesh (self, our carnal nature) leads, we will surely fail or, worse, produce a deceptive substitute that appears to be from God but is actually from our carnal nature.

God's power comes through grace and submission. The word in the Greek translated as "grace" has two possible meanings depending on the context.

> For by grace are ye saved through faith; and that not of yourselves: [it is] the gift of God: Not of works, lest any man should boast.
>
> (Ephesians 2:8-9)

In these verses, the word translated as "grace" means *un-merited favor*. In other contexts, the word translated as "grace" means *operational power*. That is God's enabling power, which He bestows upon us for His purposes.

> If ye have heard of the dispensation of the grace of God which is given me to you-ward.
>
> (Ephesians 3:2)

The grace in this verse is operational power, divine enabling, by which Paul could speak, work and minister into the lives of others for their benefit. The *Phillips* translation says, "For you must have heard how God gave me grace to become your minister." To paraphrase, God gave Paul an enabling power to become their servant. God did not give Paul divine power so he could rule (dominate) the people but so he could serve and help them (see 1 Corinthians 1:24).

God's way is opposite from the world's way. Give power to a person in the world and he or she will rule and dominate other people. Give power to a righteous-minded servant of God, however, and he or she will get behind everyone else and lift them up.

> Having then gifts differing according to the grace that is given to us, whether prophecy, [let us prophesy] according to the proportion of faith.
>
> (Romans 12:6)

The grace bestowed for the gifts mentioned in this verse is not salvation grace, because everyone is alike in salvation grace. Therefore, it must mean grace for divinely bestowed talents, abilities, operational power, and divine enabling.

> I thank my God always on your behalf, for the grace of God which is given you by Jesus Christ; That in every thing ye are enriched by him, in all utterance, and [in] all knowledge; Even as the testimony of Christ was confirmed in you: So that

ye come behind in no gift; waiting for the coming of our Lord Jesus Christ.

(1 Corinthians 1:4-7)

In this passage, the Greek word translated as "grace" is *charis*. The word for "gift" (spiritual gift) is *charisma*, which means gift of grace. The gifts of God, given by the Holy Spirit, are supernatural gifts. *Charisma* equips and enables believers.

According to the grace of God which is given unto me, as a wise masterbuilder, I have laid the foundation, and another buildeth thereon. But let every man take heed how he buildeth thereupon.

(1 Corinthians 3:10)

Through grace, Paul was equipped to lay the foundation. Only operational power could have done that. Paul was able to do specific tasks because God gave him grace, enabling power and authority.

But by the grace of God I am what I am; and his grace which [was bestowed] upon me was not in vain; but I labored more abundantly than they all; yet not I, but the grace of God which was with me.

(1 Corinthians 15:10)

In this passage, Paul was saying that he didn't make himself an apostle but that it came by grace, the favor and power of God. He pointed out that although he was given this grace, he labored more diligently than others, meaning he applied what he had been given. The grace and power of God in him produced the results.

Do you lay hands on the sick and heal them by *your* power? Do you prophesy by *your* power? Do you have faith to move mountains by *your* power? No! Jesus declared that He didn't do the work but that it was the Father in Him doing the work (see John 14:10). When we do something by the power of God, we should note that it is not us who do this work but Jesus in us.

God often chooses to use people to carry out His will, but the power and the glory are His.

Submission to the will of God is the next element of divine power. This submission is not to our will or to the will of others. We must understand how our submission to God's will releases divine power.

> Now the God of peace, that brought again from the dead our Lord Jesus, that great shepherd of the sheep, through the blood of the everlasting covenant, Make you perfect in every good work *to do his will,* working in you that which is well pleasing in his sight, through Jesus Christ; to whom [be] glory for ever and ever. Amen.
>
> (Hebrews 13:20-21, emphasis added)

God equips us according to His will to do what He wants. If we move outside of His will, the results we accomplish will be only through our human power.

> Not every one who saith unto me, Lord, Lord, shall enter into the Kingdom of heaven; but he that doeth the will of my Father which is in heaven.
>
> (Matthew 7:21)

We progress in the kingdom of God by doing the will of the Father. The advancement of the Kingdom in us is hindered every time we choose to follow our natural will. Most of the time we don't realize how costly it is to choose our will over God's will.

> I can of mine own self do nothing; as I hear, I judge: and my judgment is just; because I seek not mine own will, but the will of the Father which hath sent me.
>
> (John 5:30)

In this verse, "judge" and "judgment" mean discernment. We should infer from this that if we are not committed to do the will of God, our discernment is adversely affected.

When the light of Jesus, the burst of Shekinah glory of God, manifested to Saul of Tarsus on the road to Damascus and blinded him, he asked two of the most important questions recorded in the Bible. The answers changed the course of his life. The first question he asked was, "Lord, who are you?" Saul had the presence of mind to say "Lord" because he realized he had encountered power and authority beyond anything he had ever experienced. He heard the answer: "I am Jesus."

Then Saul asked, "Lord, what would you have me to do?" Having experienced the manifested power of God in the revelation of Jesus, he no longer desired to follow his own will. From that moment on, he lived by his decision to be ruled and led by the Holy Spirit. Saul of Tarsus turned his life around (converted).

> For I came down from heaven, not to do mine own will, but the will of him that sent me.
>
> (John 6:38)

Jesus came to earth with the express purpose of fulfilling the perfect will of the Father. We must always remember that Jesus is our pattern for motive, attitude and action.

> For it is God which worketh in you both to will and to do of [His] good pleasure.
>
> (Philippians 2:13)

We have little input into our being led by the Spirit besides making the decision to yield. When we become aware that God is working something in our hearts and we agree with it, He then releases His power into our lives. That doesn't leave room for us to glorify ourselves, as both the desire and the power come from God.

> For this cause we also, since the day we heard [it], do not cease to pray for you, and to desire that *ye might be filled with the knowledge of his will* in all wisdom and spiritual understanding; That ye might walk worthy of the Lord unto all pleasing, being fruitful in every good work, and increasing in

the knowledge of God; Strengthened with all might, according to his glorious power, unto all patience and longsuffering with joyfulness.

(Colossians 1:9-11, emphasis added)

Paul wanted the Colossians to be flooded with wisdom, revelation, and understanding of God's will. He then wanted them to conduct themselves in a manner worthy of the Lord who had saved them. Paul's desire for the Colossians applies to Christians today. It is not enough to be filled with the knowledge of His will; we must put that knowledge into practice. Only then we will be fruitful, increasing in knowledge, and on a true and steady course in God's kingdom. If we fail to seek God's will in any matter, it is because we have already decided to do what *we* want to do. This is often detrimental, sometimes dangerous.

The word "strengthened" in Colossians 1:11 means filled with strength by receiving God's power. If we discern His will and submit to it, we will produce good works. We will experience a life that is lived and operated by God's strength. We will speak words and perform miracles by the power of the Holy Spirit far beyond our natural abilities.

We can apply God's divine power even in commonplace situations. My wife and I once stopped at the home of one of our sons to deliver birthday gifts while he was out. A German shepherd was chained in the yard within reach of the front door. The dog was not friendly. She was noisy, aggressive and clearly didn't like strangers in her yard. As soon as I got out of the car, the dog barked furiously and tore around wildly. The fur from her neck to the end of her tail stood on end. Her lips curled in a snarl. My wife said, "I have an idea. Why don't you take the gifts across the street, leave them at the neighbor's house, and ask them to give them to our son when he gets home." I replied, "No! I am not subject to the dominion of this dog. I am going to leave these gifts at the front door where they belong."

When I walked to the gate, the dog became even wilder. Then the power of God and boldness rose in me. I pointed at the dog and said, "I speak to you by the power of Jesus' name. I tell you to hold your peace, shut up and don't move!" Immediately, the dog froze with her eyes fixed on something that I could not see or sense. Her tail dropped between her legs. She never looked at me as I opened the gate, walked in, hung the bag of gifts on the doorknob, turned around, walked out and closed the gate. I don't know what that dog saw, but I know that the power of God stopped her. The animal went berserk the moment I was outside the gate.

> For ye have need of patience, that, after ye have done the will
> of God, ye might receive the promise.
>
> (Hebrews 10:36)

Some Christians don't comprehend that many of God's promises are conditional. They often pray, "God, You promised..." Yet God fulfills His promises when we are diligent to seek, know, and understand His will and when we are obedient and submit to His will. If we are living our lives in Jesus, becoming like Him and doing what Holy Spirit tells us to do, God will fulfill His promises.

> I beseech you therefore, brethren, by the mercies of God, that
> ye present your bodies a living sacrifice, holy, acceptable unto
> God, which is your reasonable service. And be not conformed
> to this world; but be ye transformed by the renewing of your
> mind, that ye may prove what [is] that good, and acceptable,
> and perfect, will of God.
>
> (Romans 12:1-2)

Unlike God's will, human will is not generally good, acceptable, or perfect. As one teacher put it, there is a great difference between a "good" idea and a "God" idea. We must understand that only by becoming a living sacrifice will we determine the good, perfect, and acceptable will of God. We must lay down our will and our self-centeredness and set the government of self aside. We must yield ourselves to God and say, "Father, here am I, send me," as Isaiah did. Even then, we will still have to be cleansed so that God can send us in His perfect will, just as the seraphim had to take the coal off the altar and touch it to Isaiah's lips so that he could be cleansed to do God's will (see Isaiah 6:6-7).

> Love not the world, neither the things [that are] in the world. If any man love the world, the love of the Father is not in him. For all that [is] in the world, the lust of the flesh, and the lust of the eyes, and the pride of life, is not of the Father, but is of the world. And the world passeth away, and the lust thereof: but he that doeth the will of God abideth for ever.
>
> (1 John 2:15-17)

We will abide forever if we do the will of God. However, we can't abide with God unless we give up the world's ways and our selfishness. We can't love the world and love God. We can't make our will equal to God's will. Only Jesus can be the king in the kingdom of God.

> For the kingdom of God [is] not in word, but in power.
>
> (1 Corinthians 4:20)

Christians who operate without the power of God do not fully experience the kingdom of God. This is not to say that they are second class Christians but that they are simply underpowered. They could accomplish much more if they yielded to the will of God and ministered in the power of the Holy Spirit. This requires obedience.

Chapter 4

OBEDIENCE

Are you really obedient to the Lord? Or do you choose your own way by neglecting to ask for the wisdom to know His will?

> And it shall come to pass, if thou shalt hearken diligently unto the voice of the LORD thy God, to observe [and] to do all his commandments which I command thee this day, that the LORD thy God will set thee on high above all nations of the earth: And all these blessings shall come on thee, and overtake thee, if thou shalt hearken unto the voice of the LORD thy God.
>
> (Deuteronomy 28:1-2)

God's plan for our lives will not be accomplished without our complete obedience.

> I will instruct thee and teach thee in the way which thou shalt go: I will guide thee with mine eye. Be ye not as the horse, [or] as the mule, which have no understanding: whose mouth must be held in with bit and bridle, lest they come near unto thee.
>
> (Psalms 32:8-9)

The effectiveness of the life-changing instruction we receive from God is directly dependent on our attitude. We must be teachable, open, and willing to learn. God's guidance will not be clear to us unless we first yield to Him. It's like trying to pull a stubborn mule into a place where it doesn't want to go. It is a contest of wills. Submission to God must be the attitude of our heart. This is a choice we must consciously make, as we are not by nature teachable or yielded.

> Thou hath dealt well with thy servant, O LORD, according unto thy word. Teach me good judgment and knowledge: for I have believed thy commandments. Before I was afflicted I went astray: but now I have kept thy word. Thou [art] good, and doest good; teach me thy statutes…[It is] good for me that I have been afflicted; that I might learn thy statutes. The law of thy mouth [is] better unto me than thousands of gold and silver.
>
> (Psalm 119:65-68,71-72)

The word "afflicted" in this passage means to be set back, to be brought low, or to be corrected through experience. We don't often say, "It's a good thing that I was afflicted." Such an attitude requires something beyond ourselves. Affliction from God is not punishment. It is the act of a loving Father to a child who needs to be taught the right way.

> For they verily for a few days chastened [us] after their own pleasure; but he for our profit, that we might be partakers of his holiness. Now no chastening for the present seemeth to be joyous, but grievous; nevertheless afterward it yieldeth the peaceable fruit of righteousness unto them which are exercised thereby.
>
> (Hebrews 12:10-11)

God disciplines us so that we can share His holiness and so that we will bear the peaceable fruit of righteousness.

> O that there were such an heart in them, that they would fear me, and keep all my commandments always, that it might be well with them, and with their children for ever!
>
> (Deuteronomy 5:29)

If we do not fear and respect the Lord and keep His commandments, it will not go well with us. Our children will inherit some of our tendencies to sin (see Exodus 20:5). Authority (sovereignty) is an intrinsic attribute of God. Obedience is our proper response to His authority.

We prove our love to God not by obeying Him grudgingly as a duty but with delight in our hearts (see John 15:15). Difficult circumstances come when we resist the will of God. If we attempt to go our own way, He may stand in our way as the angel stood in the way of Balaam's donkey (see Numbers 22:22-27). If we insist on having our own way, He may allow us to have it and let us suffer the consequences.

God says that it is important to obey because obedience shows respect for Him and brings blessings. Disobedience is disrespect for God, and is sin. When we disobey, curses come upon us that give our enemy opportunities to oppress us (see Deuteronomy 28:15).

> And as they departed, Jesus began to say unto the multitudes concerning John, What went ye out into the wilderness to see? A reed shaken with the wind? But what went ye out for to see? A man clothed in soft raiment? behold, they that wear soft [clothing] are in king's houses. But what ye went out for to see? A prophet? yea, I say unto you, and more than a prophet. For this is [he], of whom it is written, Behold, I send my messenger before thy face, which shall prepare thy way before thee. Verily I say unto you, Among them that are born of women there hath not risen a greater than John the Baptist: notwithstanding he that is least in the kingdom of heaven is greater than he.
>
> (Matthew 11:7-11)

John the Baptist was about the most unusual individual anyone could ever want to meet. Jesus testified that John was the greatest man who ever lived. Yet He also said the least Christian in the kingdom of God was greater than John. Why? Although John had a prophetic anointing, he did not have Jesus dwelling within him by the Spirit. John demonstrated his obedience to

God and his separation from the religious establishment of the day by living in the wilderness. Like John, we are called to present ourselves as living sacrifices to God and not be conformed to this world. We must be so different in a righteous way that we stand out in this world as John did in his day.

If we act like worldly people, we will appear to be exactly like them, and unbelievers will conclude that Christianity is nothing special. Our behavior must send a clear message that we are different because of our obedience to God. Our attitudes, values and behaviors must support our declaration of faithfulness to Jesus.

> Wherefore Jesus also, that he might sanctify the people with his own blood, suffered without the gate. Let us go forth therefore unto him without the camp, bearing his reproach.
> (Hebrews 13:12-13)

The world tells us we are crazy to be doing all the "Christian stuff" we do. Unbelieving acquaintances invite us to join with the old crowd and have a good time. However, the Word says we must be found outside the city (the world system). We cannot be governed by the opinions of the world, or even by friends or family. If other people do not want to obey and honor God, that is their choice, but we must not allow their choice to affect our obedience to God.

> But when he saw many of the Pharisees and Sadducees come to his baptism, he said unto them, O generation of vipers, who hath warned you to flee from the wrath to come? Bring forth therefore fruits meet for repentance: And think not to say within yourselves, We have Abraham to [our] father; for I say unto you, that God is able of these stones to raise up children unto Abraham.
> (Matthew 3:7-9)

John the Baptist confronted the religious spirit of his day. When the Pharisees and Sadducees came to his baptism, he immediately recognized they wanted only to participate in another religious ritual. He questioned their motives and ordered them to depart and prove their repentance by their actions. John did not compromise his message for the prominent religious people of the day. He spoke truth and righteousness without compromise.

John declared that King Herod was living in the sin of adultery because he had wrongly married his brother's wife. His commitment to truth and righteousness cost him his life (see Matthew 14:8-10). Jesus tells us, "For whosoever will save his life shall lose it: and whosoever will lose his life for my sake shall find it" (Matthew 16:25).

> But I say unto you, Love your enemies, bless them that curse you, do good to them that hate you, and pray for them which despitefully use you, and persecute you.
>
> (Matthew 5:44)

Loving our enemies is not a divine suggestion but a requirement. God knows what happens when we take a strong and uncompromising position in obedience to His Word. Our stand brings conviction of sin to worldly people, and our example of holiness is a testimony against them. Jesus said that if the world hates Him, it would also hate us (see John 15:18).

Much of the Christian Church today expends great effort and resources to make itself acceptable to the world. However, God intends the Church to be different. He never meant for the chasm to be bridged; He meant for it to be jumped. Following Christ is a commitment—a flying leap—that cannot be reversed in midair.

> John answered and said, A man can receive nothing, except it be given him from heaven. Ye yourselves bear me witness, that I said, I am not the Christ, but that I am sent before him. He that hath the bride is the bridegroom: but the friend of the bridegroom, which standeth and heareth him, rejoiceth greatly because of the bridegroom's voice: this my joy therefore is fulfilled. *He must increase, but I [must] decrease.* He that cometh from above is above all: he that is of the earth

is earthly, and speaketh of the earth: he that cometh from
heaven is above all.

(John 3:27-31, emphasis added)

John rejected popularity, though many people considered him
to be a great man and a prophet. When people tried to make him
someone special, he always told them that he was not the one
they should be seeking. He told them that they should be seeking
Jesus, the Anointed One. John didn't draw people to himself but
pointed them toward Christ.

Humble yourselves therefore under the mighty hand of God,
that he may exalt you in due time.

(1 Peter 5:6)

God tells us to humble ourselves. We must make that decision and choose the low place. We must choose not to seek a seat
at the head table but determine to take the place and identity of
a servant. If we exalt ourselves, God will humble us. It is much
easier to humble ourselves than to have God allow humiliation
to come.

For me to live [is] Christ, and to die [is] gain.

(Philippians 1:21)

Paul had learned that true life is in Jesus and that our worldly
life has no lasting value.

I am crucified with Christ: nevertheless I live; yet not I, but
Christ liveth in me: and the life which I now live in the flesh
I live by the faith of the Son of God, who loved me, and gave
himself for me.

(Galatians 2:20)

Some believe that the word "faith" in this passage should
be understood as "faithfulness." Paul wanted to stop living a
self-centered life so he could have the life of Jesus. Therefore, he

lived for Jesus, in Jesus, and through Jesus. As a result, his life manifested Jesus. God calls us to live the same way.

> And Moses was content to dwell with the man; and he gave Moses Zipporah, his daughter.
>
> (Exodus 2:21)

The life of Moses offers another example of being obedient to God. Moses didn't decide to remain in the desert, but he was content to remain there. Contrast Moses' attitude with that of Paul:

> But what things were gain to me, those I counted loss for Christ. Yea doubtless, and I count all things [but] loss for the excellency of the knowledge of Christ Jesus my Lord: for whom I have suffered the loss of all things, and do count them [but] dung, that I may win Christ.
>
> (Philippians 3:7-8)

Paul did not settle for partial commitment. He released everything in his old life. Jesus was his one and only goal. Moses had a problem: He was content to remain where he was.

> And Moses said unto God, Who [am] I, that I should go unto Pharaoh, and that I should bring forth the children of Israel out of Egypt?
>
> (Exodus 3:11)

In 2 Corinthians 3:5, Paul writes, "Not that we are sufficient of ourselves to think any thing as of ourselves; but our sufficiency [is] of God." If God asks us to do something, we should be aware that we are able to do it *because God gives us the enabling along with the call.*

Moses feared retaliation from the consequences of his earlier life in Egypt, and this also hindered him from obeying God.

> And the LORD said unto Moses in Midian, Go, return into Egypt; for all the men are dead which sought thy life.
>
> (Exodus 4:19)

> The fear of man bringeth a snare: But whoso putteth his trust
> in the Lord shall be safe.
>
> (Proverbs 29:25)

If we fear man we will be trapped, but if we put our trust in the Lord, we will be saved. We should reject caution rooted in the fear of man but be attentive to caution coming from the fear of the Lord.

> And Moses spake before the LORD, saying Behold the chil-
> dren of Israel have not hearkened unto me; how then shall
> Pharaoh hear me, who [am] of uncircumcised lips?
>
> (Exodus 6:12)

Even after Moses had several conversations with God, he continued to confess belief in his own limitations rather than in what God could do.

> But be ye doers of the word, and not hearers only, deceiv-
> ing your own selves. For if any be a hearer of the word, and
> not a doer, he is like unto a man beholding his natural face
> in a glass: For he beholdeth himself, and goeth his way, and
> straightway forgetteth what manner of man he was. But
> whoso looketh into the perfect law of liberty, and continueth
> [therein], he being not a forgetful hearer, but a doer of the
> work, this man shall be blessed in his deed.
>
> (James 1:22-25)

We can lose our opportunities by focusing on our personal limitations. However, if we lift our eyes from our limitations and look on God who has called us, we are reminded that through Him we are able to do all things (see Philippians 4:13). If we want blessings from God, we must do what God asks of us without procrastination and without argument about what we can't do or don't want to do.

Once when I was praying, the Lord gave me three Scripture references. When I read the Scriptures, I wept and asked the Lord what I had done that would cause Him to speak so strongly against me. He answered, "These are not for you. They are for [He named a Christian leader that I knew well]. I want you to take these verses to him and tell him that I sent you to him."

My reaction was that I didn't want anything to do with this assignment. I argued that I had no spiritual authority to correct this man. I complained that the only possible outcome that I could expect was for the man to become upset and angry. Yet the Lord did not relent in His gentle pressing for me to obey. Day after day, I resisted and told the Lord every reason I could think of as to why this was not a good idea. Day after day, the Lord called me to submit to His will. Finally, after a week of resisting, the person to whom God wanted me to speak left on vacation. I breathed a sigh of relief. I thought that I now wouldn't have to confront this man.

Throughout the month, thoughts of these verses would occasionally return, but I dismissed them. Then the day came when the man's vacation was over. I was scheduled to be in a meeting with him in the evening. At lunchtime while I was reading and praying, the thought of taking the Scriptures to him again came back strongly. Again I resisted. Suddenly, all became black and silent around me. I was not conscious of any presence of life. I was isolated in utter blackness, and I was frightened. I cried out to God to come and rescue me from this terrifying experience.

Through the blackness, the voice of the Lord came to me and said two words that eliminated all further resistance: "Remember Jonah?" I decided to do what the Lord had required of me and take the Scriptures to the person. He did get angry, but it no longer mattered to me. My responsibility was simply to obey God and deliver the message, not to convince the person or attempt to validate myself.

Some days later, I dared to ask the Lord about the blackness. He told me that I had experienced the outer darkness. My disobedience had brought unpleasant consequences. Resisting obedience is disobedience.

A speaker once asked, "When was the last time you did something for the first time?" This is a profound question. If we do not have a relatively up-to-date answer, it is likely that we have settled into a comfort zone. When we seek our comfort, we are not seeking God's will. Israel's experience at the Red Sea is an example of this:

> And the LORD spake unto Moses, saying, Speak unto the children of Israel, that they turn and encamp before Pi-hahiroth, between Migdol and the sea, over against Baal-zephon: before it shall ye encamp by the sea. For Pharaoh will say of the children of Israel, They [are] entangled in the land, the wilderness hath shut them in. And I will harden Pharaoh's heart, that he shall follow after them; and I will be honored upon Pharaoh, and upon all his host; that the Egyptians may know that I [am] the Lord. And they did so.
>
> (Exodus 14:1-4)

God announced the objectives of His plan to Israel and said He was going to be honored over the Egyptians. He told the Israelites in advance that it was His plan to have the Egyptians pursue them. He gave them His Word, but not the details.

> And when the Pharaoh drew nigh, the children of Israel lifted up their eyes, and, behold, the Egyptians marched after them; and they were sore afraid: and the children of Israel cried out unto the LORD. And they said unto Moses, Because [there were] no graves in Egypt, has thou taken us away to die in the wilderness? wherefore hast thou dealt thus with us, to carry us forth out of Egypt? [Is] not this the word that we did tell thee in Egypt, saying, Let us alone, that we may serve the Egyptians? For [it had been] better for us to serve the Egyptians, than that we should die in the wilderness.
>
> (Exodus 14:10-12)

God gave the Israelites advance information. He revealed signs and wonders to them during the ten plagues that were visited upon Egypt. Despite this, the moment things appeared to go wrong, the people panicked. They asked God why He had taken them away from their predictable lives as slaves to bring them into a freedom filled with risk and uncertainty. If we focus our eyes on circumstances instead of on God, we will live subdued or even depressed lives.

God later challenged His people to go into the Promised Land and possess their inheritance:

> And Caleb stilled the people before Moses, and said, Let us go up at once, and possess it; for we are well able to overcome it. But the men who went up with him said, We be not able to go up against the people; for they [are] stronger than we. And they brought up an evil report of the land which they had searched unto the children of Israel, saying, The land, through which we have gone to search it, [is] a land that eateth up the inhabitants thereof; and all the people that we saw in it [are] men of a great stature. And there we saw the giants, the sons of Anak, [which come] of the giants: and we were in our own sight as grasshoppers, and so we were in their sight.
>
> (Numbers 13:30-33)

The giants didn't prevent the Israelites from entering the Promised Land—the grasshoppers did! The people saw themselves as grasshoppers because of their lack of faith in God. Fear rooted in unbelief kept them out. Unbelief is the refusal to believe the truth; it involves the will.

> Take heed, brethren, lest there be in any of you an evil heart of unbelief, in departing from the living God. But exhort one another daily, while it is called Today; lest any of you be hardened through the deceitfulness of sin. For we are made partakers of Christ, if we hold the beginning of our confidence steadfast unto the end; While it is said, Today if ye will hear his voice, harden not your hearts, as in the provocation. For some, when they had heard, did provoke: howbeit not all that came out of Egypt by Moses. But with whom was he grieved forty years? was it not with them that had sinned, whose carcasses fell in the wilderness? And to whom sware he that they should not enter into his rest, but to them that believed not? So we see that they could not enter in because of unbelief.
>
> (Hebrews 3:12-19)

Unbelief inhibits obedience. If we do not believe that God *enables* us to do what He has *assigned* us to do and base our decision to obey on what *we* think *we* can do, we will often fail to obey. God is creative in advancing His kingdom, solving our dilemmas and defeating our enemies. He does not require that we understand, only that we believe His Word and His promise to be faithful.

> Thus saith the LORD; Cursed [be] the man that trusteth in man, and maketh flesh his arm, and whose heart departeth from the LORD. For he shall be like the heath in the desert, and shall not see when good cometh; but shall inhabit the parched places in the wilderness, [in] a salt land and not inhabited. Blessed [is] the man that trusteth in the LORD and whose hope the LORD is. For he shall be as a tree planted by the waters, and [that] spreadeth out her roots by the river, and shall not see when heat cometh, but her leaf shall be green; and shall not careful in the year of drought, neither shall cease from yielding fruit.
>
> (Jeremiah 17:5-8)

We have the choice of whether we will trust in what we think we can do for ourselves, in what we think other people can do for us, or in what we think the Lord can do for us. Our hope and trust must be centered in the Lord. Difficulties will come and the flesh will fail, but God will keep us, carry us and bring us through. God's provision may arrive at the eleventh hour and in the fifty-ninth minute, but He will never be late, and He will never fail us.

> Only be thou strong and very courageous, that thou mayest observe to do according to all the law, which Moses my servant commanded thee: turn not from it to the right hand or to the left, that thou mayest prosper whithersoever thou goest. This book of the law shall not depart out of thy mouth; but thou shalt meditate therein day and night, *that thou mayest observe to do according to all that is written therein*: for then thou shalt make thy way prosperous, and then thou shalt have

good success. Have not I commanded thee? Be strong and of a
good courage; be not afraid, neither be thou dismayed: for the
Lord thy God is with thee whithersoever thou goest.

(Joshua 1:7-9, emphasis added)

When God gives us a directive, we must set our hearts and
minds to do it exactly the way He has instructed. We can't turn
aside to carnal alternatives or yield to fear or dismay. "Dismay"
in this sense means to be broken down or prostrated by violence,
confusion, or fear.

When Joshua led Israel across the Jordan River into the
Promised Land, God told him that the priests, bearing the Ark
of the Covenant, were to go ahead of the people and stand in
the river though the Jordan was in flood (see Joshua 3:13-17).
The instant the priests obeyed (committed themselves), the river
parted. The Israelites crossed over on dry ground, just as they
had crossed over the Red Sea when they had come out of Egypt.
Joshua chose obedience despite the risk of failure. He put his
reputation on the line for God.

We must *get our feet wet* by making a commitment and a
decision to obey what the Lord is asking us to do before He will
act. The world bargains before making a commitment, but God
tells us to believe and commit and then He will demonstrate His
power. Many times, the fear of loss of respectability or reputation
will prevent us from taking a leap of faith. It has been said that
we can have human respectability or we can have the anointing,
but we can't have both.

In James 3:17, the author speaks of a wisdom from above that
is easily entreated. To be "easily entreated" means to be compliant
and ready to obey. Our attitude should be, "Lord, I have decided
to do Your will even before I know what Your will is." Obedience
proves a loving relationship with Jesus.

For this is the love of God, that we keep his commandments:
and his commandments are not grievous.

(1 John 5:3)

> He that hath my commandments, and keepeth them, he it is
> that loveth me: and he that loveth me shall be loved of my
> Father, and I will love him, and will manifest myself to him.
>
> (John 15:21)

First Samuel 15:23 states that rebellion is as witchcraft and stubbornness is as idolatry. These are important spiritual maxims. I believe the Hebrew suggests that stubbornness is the idolatry of self. We cannot rebel against God or stubbornly resist His will without sinning and experiencing the consequences. We must not allow our reasoning to substitute worldly logic in place of simply obeying God's directives.

> And when they had brought them, they set them before the
> council: and the high priest asked them, Saying, Did not we
> straitly command you that ye should not teach in this name?
> and, behold, ye have filled Jerusalem with your doctrine, and
> intend to bring this man's blood upon us. Then Peter and
> the other apostles answered and said, We ought to obey God
> rather than men.
>
> (Acts 5:27-29)

Jesus' disciples chose God over the world. They were brought before the religious authorities for preaching about Christ in the Temple. They were beaten, threatened, set free, and again ordered to stop preaching Jesus. Yet this did not deter them from following the Lord's instructions.

> And they departed from the presence of the council, rejoicing
> that they were counted worthy to suffer shame for his name.
> And daily in the temple, and in every house, they ceased not
> to teach and preach Jesus Christ.
>
> (Acts 5:41-42)

In John 12:42-43, Jesus described a problem among believers. Many priests believed in Christ but wouldn't publicly proclaim Him. They were afraid they would be cast out of the synagogue and lose their favored positions. Jesus said they loved the praise of man more than they loved the praise of God.

In Galatians 5:16-17, Paul states that the flesh and the Spirit are incompatible and cannot peacefully coexist. Each seeks to be preeminent. Flesh, aided by Satan, is against us, but God, by His Spirit, is for us. Our decision determines the winner. We must decide to be obedient and then be consistent in our obedience.

There are two different kinds of decisions: A capital D decision followed by a period and a lowercase d decision followed by a comma. A [Decision.] means nothing precedes the decision and nothing follows. A [decision,] means that the decision is influenced by something that came first and is modified by something that follows. The first is a clear decision; the second is an attempt to negotiate with God, which is never successful. We need to consider what type of decision we are making when we choose to obey God. Are we trying to design a way of escape if things don't work out our way or to our benefit?

Deuteronomy 30:6 tells us that God is not looking for circumcised flesh but for a circumcised heart. This is a heart (motive, attitude) in which resistance to God has been cut away by an act of the will. It is an attitude in which we determine that God's will is going to be the most important thing in life and that we are going to do things His way. Circumcision of the flesh means nothing if the heart is not right before God. Relationship with God is based on heart attitude and continuing decisions to deny self, not on any external conformance to rules. We are warned that we must have inward transformation, not outward pretense.

> For he is not a Jew, which is one outwardly; neither is that circumcision, which is outward in the flesh: But he is a Jew, which is one inwardly; and circumcision is that of the heart, in the spirit, and not in the letter; whose praise is not of men, but of God.
>
> (Romans 2:28-29)

We read in Joshua 24:15, "And if it seem evil unto you to serve the LORD, choose you this day whom you will serve; whether the gods which your fathers served that were on the other side of the flood, or the gods of the Amorites, in whose land ye dwell: but as for me and my house, we will serve the LORD." We must make a commitment to follow the Lord that we honor despite circumstances and without regard for risk or cost—especially regarding the attitudes or opinions of others.

> And he went a little further, and fell on his face, and prayed, saying, O my Father, if it be possible, let this cup pass from me: *nevertheless not as I will, but as thou wilt.*
>
> (Matthew 26:39, emphasis added)

I once heard it said that the word "nevertheless" in this passage could be understood to mean "always the more." Jesus, our perfect example, withheld nothing from the Father. I prayed to the Lord, asking, "What is the extent of the obedience You expect from a believer?" I do not to this day know whether what I saw was physically real or an open vision by the Spirit, but His answer came in big, bold, black letters on the front of an otherwise all white truck: "**WHATEVER IT TAKES.**" One thing it takes is holiness.

Chapter 5

HOLINESS

Are you convinced that personal holiness is an inescapable necessity? Do you believe that it is attainable? If so, are you pursuing it with all your might?

> And ye shall be holy unto me: for I the LORD [am] holy, and have severed you from [other] people, that ye should be mine.
>
> (Leviticus 20:26)

In the Old Testament, *Jehovah Qanna* is one of the names used for God. It means the Lord whose name is Jealous. "Jealous" as used here means vigilant, as in guarding a possession. God is jealous of the people and objects that are exclusively His. When He states in this verse that He has severed His people from others, He is saying that they are holy. Holiness means to be separated unto the Lord and set apart for His purposes.

> Having therefore these promises, dearly beloved, let us cleanse ourselves from all filthiness of the flesh and spirit, perfecting holiness in the fear of God.
>
> (2 Corinthians 7:1)

"Perfecting" means to make fulfilled or to make complete. The fear of the Lord is not panic and terror but reverence, submission, and awesome respect. If we awesomely respect, honor, and submit to the Lord, we should be seeking to be thoroughly cleansed and completely set apart unto God—in other words, made holy. God removes our carnal nature (with our consent) and imparts His nature. As we are transformed into the nature of Jesus, we become more set apart from the world and more separated unto God. We become holy.

Sanctification is the process of being transformed into God's nature. The word "godly" is defined in *Funk and Wagnall's Dictionary* as "filled with the love of God." The word "godliness," according to *Thayer's Lexicon,* is "reverence, respect, and dutiful. It denotes that piety which, characterized by a God-ward attitude, does what is well pleasing to Him."

> Therefore if any man [be] in Christ, [he] is a new creature: old things are passed away; behold, all things are become new.
>
> (2 Corinthians 5:17)

Becoming new in Christ is a provisional truth that we have not yet fully experienced. Some of our old nature remains. However, because the Word of God is true, it must be possible for us to become a completely new creature [creation]. In this life, we will become as much like Jesus as we want to be.

> Sanctify them through thy truth: thy word is truth.
>
> (John 17:17)

God the Father is one source of sanctification. Jesus asked His Father to sanctify the believers through the Father's truth.

> And the very God of peace sanctify you *wholly*; and [I pray God] your whole spirit and soul and body be preserved blameless unto the coming of our Lord Jesus Christ. Faithful [is] he that calleth you, who also will do [it].
>
> (1 Thessalonians 5:23-24, emphasis added)

"Wholly" means totally, absolutely perfect, perfectly complete and fulfilled. Paul also prayed that Christ would be formed in us (see Galatians 4:19). Paul said he would continue praying until sanctification was complete.

> Being confident of this very thing, that he which hath begun a good work in you will perform [it] until the day of Jesus Christ.
>
> (Philippians 1:6)

God the Father is involved in our sanctification, but the Word tells us that Jesus is also involved.

> Wherefore Jesus also, that he might sanctify the people with his own blood, suffered without the gate.
>
> (Hebrews 13:12)

God the Father sanctifies us by His truth. Jesus sanctifies us by His blood.

> But of him are ye in Christ Jesus, who of God is made unto us wisdom, and righteousness, and sanctification, and redemption.
>
> (1 Corinthians 1:30)

We are called (summoned) to be saints, which means holy ones. The Holy Spirit is active in our sanctification.

> Elect according to the foreknowledge of God the Father, through sanctification of the Spirit, unto obedience and sprinkling of the blood of Jesus Christ: Grace unto you, and peace, be multiplied.
>
> (1 Peter 1:2)

We are sanctified through the Holy Spirit to obedience. Jesus was perfectly obedient to the will of the Father. He is the pattern that we are to follow.

> And such were some of you: but ye are washed, but ye are
> sanctified, but ye are justified in the name of the Lord Jesus,
> and by the Spirit of our God.
>
> (1 Corinthians 6:11)

We are sanctified in the name of Jesus. The phrase "in the name of" refers to the authority of Jesus.

> But we are bound to give thanks always to God for you, breth-
> ren beloved of the Lord, because God hath from the begin-
> ning chosen you to salvation through sanctification of the
> Spirit and belief of the truth.
>
> (2 Thessalonians 2:13)

"Salvation" in this verse refers to forgiveness of sin and the development of a holy life. If God the Father, God the Son and God the Holy Spirit are working on sanctification, it must be of vital importance. Sanctification produces the likeness of Jesus in us. It changes outward our expressions and the inward workings, motives, and attitudes of our hearts. It creates new responses and new reactions to our circumstances. It alters our behavior and changes our value system. It leads to new friends and new purposes. It gives us a new kind of power that makes us different from worldly people.

If we allow the process of sanctification to work in us, it will produce a completely new person. The world will see us as noticeably different. People will ask questions such as, "What is it about you? Why do you glow like that? Why didn't you get upset when that person offended you? Where did you get the power to heal that person?"

As believers, we can only be an effective light to this world if we shine brightly enough to attract people who live in darkness (see Matthew 4:16). This will cause them to say, "Wait a minute, it's dark over here, but it's light over there. Let me go find out what that's all about." If we are to be bright lights, we should seek to be 100-watt bulbs rather than 30- or 60-watt ones (see Matthew 13:8).

> For there are three that bear record in heaven, the Father, the
> Word, and the Holy Ghost: and these three are one. And there
> are three that bear witness in earth, the spirit, and the water,
> and the blood: and these three agree in one.
>
> (1 John 5:7-8)

God is one (see Deuteronomy 6:4), but He reveals Himself
in three distinct persons. We know the Father in creation, the
Son in redemption, and the Spirit in orchestration. The Spirit,
the water and the blood are all part of sanctification that brings
holiness.

> How much more shall the blood of Christ, who through the
> eternal Spirit offered himself without spot to God, purge your
> conscience from dead works to serve the living God?
>
> (Hebrews 9:14)

I define "dead works" as everything we do that God doesn't
ask us to do. Only those works assigned by the Spirit and accomplished by the Spirit are living works. Everything born of
the carnal nature breeds corruption and death (see Galatians
6:7-8). Only what we do by the Spirit and at the initiation of
the Holy Spirit will endure and pass the test of fire. Gold, silver
and precious gems (living works) will pass through the fire and
come out purified (see 1 Corinthians 3:11-15). These are the
works of the Spirit.

One day, the Holy Spirit said to me, "Get ready for the firestorm." I pondered this for several days but could not gain any
understanding as to what it meant. Finally, I prayed, "Lord, I
don't know how to get ready for a firestorm." He answered, "Get
rid of all the combustibles in your life."

The Scriptures identify three things that will be burned. First,
dead works that produce wood, hay, and stubble (see 1 Corinthians 3:12). Second, chaff, which I understand to be character
defects (see Matthew 3:12). Third, unfruitful branches, which
I believe are activities or programs that are not producing fruit
that remains (see John 15:16).

Husbands, love your wives, even as Christ also loved the church, and gave himself for it; That he might sanctify and cleanse it with the washing of the water by the word, That he might present it to himself a glorious church, not having spot, or wrinkle, or any such thing; but that it should be holy and without blemish.

(Ephesians 5:25-27)

A "laver" was a washstand in the Outer Court of the Tabernacle of Moses that was made of highly polished brass and filled with water. It served as an effective mirror. When a priest stood over this washstand, he saw himself the way he really was. He washed his hands and feet, signifying his washing away the defilement of the world from everything that he had touched and where he had walked. After he was cleansed, he could enter into the first covered part of the tabernacle, the Holy Place, and perform the rituals of worship and sacrifice to the Lord.

Peter saith unto him, Thou shalt never wash my feet. Jesus answered him, *If I wash thee not, thou hast no part with me.* Simon Peter saith unto him, Lord, not my feet only, but also my hands and my head.

(John 13:8-9, emphasis added)

We are a royal priesthood, a holy nation set apart unto God (see 1 Peter 2:9). We must have our hands, feet and heads washed by the Word of God to cleanse us from the defilement and influence of the world.

And thou has sent me into the world, even so have I also sent them into the world. And for their sakes I sanctify myself, that they also might be sanctified through the truth.

(John 17:18-19)

The Spirit of the Lord is the Spirit of Truth, and He will guide us into all truth (see John 16:13). In John 8:32, Jesus says, "And ye shall know the truth, and the truth shall make you free." God's truth permeating our lives brings freedom and separation from sin to righteousness (see Romans 6:16). Loving the truth is the only effective preventative for deception (see 2 Thessalonians 2:10).

> Then said he, Lo, I come to do thy will, O God. He taketh away the first, that he may establish the second. By the which will we are sanctified through the offering of the body of Jesus Christ once for all.
>
> (Hebrews 10:9-10)

This verse says we *are* sanctified, meaning that this process has been accomplished. The completion of sanctification is contained within the sacrifice of Jesus, but sanctification is an ongoing process. Again, we encounter an apparent dichotomy: Jesus' sacrifice on the cross is the *provision* for sanctification (see 1 Corinthians 1:30), but we must *experience* the process that applies it. This is not a contradiction.

> For when Moses had spoken every precept to all the people according to the law, he took the blood of calves and of goats, with water, and scarlet wool, and hyssop, and sprinkled both the book, and all the people, Saying, This is the blood of the testament which God hath enjoined unto you. Moreover he sprinkled with blood both the tabernacle, and all the vessels of the ministry.
>
> (Hebrews 9:19-21)

The blood to which the author of Hebrews refers was applied to seal and complete sanctification. It means the blood of Jesus must be applied not only for the forgiveness of sin but also to the very attitudes of our hearts and to the very center of our being. Some people think that because they are saved, all they have to do is hang on until Jesus returns. They are missing a major component of Christian life. Salvation is only the beginning. Sanctification carries us further into the kingdom of God and to Christlikeness.

> Let us draw near with a true heart in full assurance of faith,
> having our hearts sprinkled from an evil conscience, and our
> bodies washed with pure water.
>
> (Hebrews 10:22)

Thayer's Lexicon says, "This refers to the soul as distinguishing what is morally good and bad." The applied Word prompts us to do what is good and shun what is bad (see Philippians 1:9-10). This means we make righteous choices based on internal application of the Word of God. Having an "evil conscience" means we believe that we can follow our human will without consequences. We have not been called to follow our own way; we have been called to obey the Lord.

Being "washed with pure water" refers to the water of the Word. The Word of God must wash our bodies as well as our minds. He wants the Word applied to our lives—not only heard only but also applied!

> How much more shall the blood of Christ, who through the
> eternal Spirit offered himself without spot to God, purge your
> conscience from the dead works to serve the living God?
>
> (Hebrews 9:14)

The theologian Terry Fullam once said that if he looked far enough—and he probably wouldn't have to look far—he could find someone who would make him look good if he measured himself against that person. However, he also said, "That is deception and hypocrisy. If I am ever to walk in truth and light, I have to look to Jesus and compare myself to Him." When we compare ourselves to Jesus, we usually don't look so good.

> For this is the will of God, [even] your sanctification, that
> ye should abstain from fornication: That every one of you
> should know how to possess his vessel in sanctification and
> honor: Not in the lust of concupiscence, even as the Gen-
> tiles which know not God: That no [man] go beyond and

defraud his brother in [any] matter: because that the Lord
[is] the avenger of all such, as we also have forewarned you
and testified. For God hath not called us unto uncleanness,
but unto holiness. He therefore that despiseth, despiseth not
man, but God, who hath also given unto us his Holy Spirit.

(1 Thessalonians 4:3-5)

Sanctification not only works the nature of God into us but
also involves working the old carnal nature out of us. Sanctification involves removing fornication, evil desires, defrauding (a
form of dishonesty) or taking unfair advantage out of our nature.
Jesus must increase and we (self, carnal nature) must decrease
(see John 3:30).

Nevertheless the foundation of God standeth sure, having
this seal, the Lord knoweth them that are his. And, let every one that nameth the name of Christ depart from iniquity.
But in a great house there are not only vessels of gold and
of silver, but also of wood and of earth; and some to honor,
and some to dishonor. If a man therefore purge himself from
these, he shall be a vessel unto honor, sanctified, and meet for
the master's use, [and] prepared unto every good work.

(2 Timothy 2: 19-21)

A parable is told of a table that has been set for two in a quiet,
secluded dining area, but only one guest is expected. At one end
of the table, the place is set with a full service of the finest gold.
At the other end, the place is set very sparsely with common
wooden service. The wooden pieces are marred, discolored and
scratched.

However, a closer inspection reveals that the gold setting
is encrusted with spoiled food and crawling with insects. The
wooden pieces, on the other hand, have been scoured and are
clean despite their outward appearance. The guest soon arrives;
it is Jesus. Which place setting do you think He will choose?

So it is with us. The Lord chooses not that which has external
appeal, valued by humanity, but that which has been prepared by

the Spirit for Him alone. As we depart from iniquity and purge ourselves from unrighteous words, thoughts and deeds, we become more appropriate for the Master's use. The end result of sanctification is that we are set apart, prepared, fulfilled, finished, and identified as belonging to God.

> Draw nigh to God, and he will draw nigh to you. Cleanse [your] hands, [ye] sinners; and purify [your] hearts, [ye] double minded. Be afflicted, and mourn, and weep: let your laughter be turned to mourning and [your] joy to heaviness. Humble yourselves in the sight of the Lord, and he shall lift you up. Speak not evil one of another, brethren. He that speaketh evil of [his] brother, and judgeth his brother, speaketh evil of the law, and judgeth the law: but if thou judge the law, thou art not a doer of the law, but a judge. There is one lawgiver, who is able to save and to destroy: who art thou that judgest another?
>
> (James 4:8-12)

The phrase "to cleanse our hands" means to wash away involvement with sin and separate ourselves from wrong relationships. We often hear even worldly people express dissociation from something as having "washed their hands" of it. Pontius Pilate attempted to separate himself from the crucifixion of Jesus by a public display of washing his hands.

We must purify our hearts. Our "heart" includes our thoughts, attitudes, and motives. It is not sufficient in the sight of God to have an external appearance of holiness without having the internal parts of the vessel cleansed (see Matthew 23:27-28). We must turn our false joy into mourning and our careless laughter into wailing. As James says, we are not what we think we are. If we see ourselves through God's eyes, we will find that we should be crying out to God instead of feeling complacent.

James also states that we should choose humility and cease judging. One of the evidences of sanctification is that we no longer judge others. We are to humble ourselves before God. Pointing the accusing finger of judgment at others reveals self-righteousness, which is rooted in pride.

> Teaching us that, denying ungodliness and worldly lusts, we
> should live soberly, righteously, and godly, in this present
> world.
>
> (Titus 2:12)

In this passage, Paul admonishes us to deny ungodliness.
"Deny" means to disavow, to reject and to stand against. We
must make a firm decision against the enticements of the world
and our carnal nature. We must "mortify the deeds of the flesh"
(Romans 8:13).

> I exhort therefore, that, first of all, supplications, prayers, in-
> tercessions, [and] giving of thanks, be made for all men; For
> Kings, and [for] all that are in authority; that we may lead a
> quiet and peaceable life in all godliness and honesty. For this
> [is] good and acceptable in the sight of God our Savior; Who
> will have all men to be saved, and to come unto the knowl-
> edge of the truth.
>
> (1 Timothy 2:1-4)

Holiness is the objective; sanctification is the process, and
godliness is the external evidence that we have been transformed
into Christlikeness. This is God's purpose for two reasons: One
is for our own quietness and peace, and the second is to attract
the lost to Christ in us through our example of His nature.

> But refuse profane and old wives' fables, and exercise thyself
> [rather] unto godliness. For bodily exercise profiteth little:
> but godliness is profitable unto all things, having promise of
> the life that now is, and of that which is to come. This [is] a
> faithful saying and worthy of all acceptation.
>
> (1 Timothy 4:7-9)

Godliness is part of God's promise that we have both the life
that is now and that life which is to come. Sanctification produces holiness, which is the character of God formed in us. We
shouldn't just wait complacently until the next age comes and
say, "I'll never be perfect until I get home to Jesus." This is not a

true statement. We are to be perfected, made holy and complete in *this* life. It is attainable! The Word declares it!

> Herein is our love made perfect, that we may have boldness in the day of judgment: because as he is, *so are we in this world.*
> (1 John 4:17, emphasis added)

Excusing our behavior or failing to make a committed effort is evidence that we have not made a firm decision to press on into personal holiness. Perhaps we are trying to hold on to things that we should let go.

> If any man teach otherwise, and consent not to wholesome words, [even] the words of our Lord Jesus Christ, and to the doctrine which is according to godliness; He is proud, knowing nothing, but doting about questions and strifes of words, whereof cometh envy, strife, railings, evil surmisings, Perverse disputings of men of corrupt minds, and destitute of the truth, supposing that gain is godliness: from such withdraw thyself. But godliness with contentment is great gain. For we brought nothing into [this] world, [and it is] certain we can carry nothing out.
> (1 Timothy 6:3-7)

Some people perform work in the name of God but with the wrong motives. This Scripture lists several manifestations of our carnal nature that will reveal these wrong motives. The problem is in thinking that godliness is for gain and that we will get something out of it for ourselves. Paul makes the point that those who pursue godliness for this aim are corrupt in their inmost beings.

We shouldn't seek to be godly so God will bless us and makes us rich or healthy. We should be committed in our hearts to be godly even if we are poor and troubled and of apparently no great honor or esteem. No matter where we are, what our station in life is, or what we own, we should still have the determination to be as godly as we are able to be in Christ Jesus (see Colossians 1:28).

For the love of money is the root of all evil: which while some coveted after, they have erred from the faith, and pierced themselves through with many sorrows. But thou, O man of God, flee these things; and follow after righteousness, godliness, faith, love, patience, meekness.

(1 Timothy 6:10-11)

The phrase "follow after" in this passage means to pursue or to press toward. It isn't a leisurely walk down the street; it is hot pursuit. It is action showing commitment based on a decision.

According as his divine power hath given unto us all things that [pertain] unto life and godliness, through the knowledge of him that hath called us to glory and virtue: Whereby are given unto us exceeding great and precious promises: that by these ye might be partakers of the divine nature, having escaped the corruption that is in the world through lust.

(2 Peter 1:3-4)

God imparts His divine power to enable us to comprehend His promises and then to apprehend them. This process produces the divine nature. We cannot relax and say, "I've got the promises, praise the Lord" or talk or sing about them but do nothing about them. To receive God's promises, we must meet His conditions and pray those promises into our lives: "Father, this is what You promised, and this is what I want. Let's make it happen. What do You want me to do? How do I yield to You?"

That ye be not slothful, but followers of them who through faith and patience inherit the promises.

(Hebrews 6:12)

Holiness is an attribute of God. It cannot be attained through rules, regulations, or legalism but only by the inner working of the Holy Spirit with the active cooperation and participation of the believer. Holiness is so important that the Father, the Son, and the Holy Spirit together work it into us. We should understand that holiness is extraordinarily valuable, to be strongly desired, and that we should earnestly seek it so that we can live righteously.

Chapter 6

RIGHTEOUSNESS

Do you now understand that God would much rather have you be righteous than right? Is your righteousness only of God? Or are you self-righteous?

> Behold, the days come, saith the LORD, that I will raise unto David a righteous Branch, and a King shall reign and prosper, and shall execute judgment and justice on the earth. In his days Judah shall be saved, and Israel shall dwell safely: and this [is] his name whereby he shall be called, THE LORD OUR RIGHTEOUSNESS.
>
> (Jer. 23:56)

Being righteous means to have right standing with God. New Testament writers often remind us that we have no righteousness of our own. The only righteousness we have is that which has been imputed to us because of Jesus' death on the cross.

> Clouds and darkness are round about him; righteousness and judgment are the habitation of his throne.
>
> (Ps. 97:2)

God's government is found where righteousness and right judgment (justice) exists. If we are to live in the manifest presence of the Lord, we must live in righteousness.

> For the kingdom of God is not meat and drink; but righteousness, and peace, and joy in the Holy Ghost.
>
> (Rom. 14:17)

We will never fully experience the kingdom of God if we don't live righteously under the direction and control of the Holy Spirit.

> The LORD [is] righteousness in all his ways, and holy in all his works.
>
> (Ps. 145:17)

God does nothing that is unrighteous. Everything about Him—including His decisions, His actions and His words—are righteous. Therefore, it is never proper for a Christian to say to the Lord, "You're not fair," as this comes from a wrong spirit.

> According to thy name, O God, so is thy praise unto the ends of the earth; thy right hand is full of righteousness.
>
> (Ps. 48:10)

The right hand of God signifies authority and power. Righteousness is an attribute of God that never diminishes and never changes. Where righteousness is established, God's authority and power are expressed.

> LORD, who shall abide in thy tabernacle? who shall dwell in thy holy hill? He that walketh uprightly, and worketh righteousness, and speaketh the truth in his heart. [He that] back biteth not with his tongue, nor doeth evil to his neighbor, nor taketh up a reproach against his neighbor. In whose eyes a vile person is condemned; but he honoreth them that fear the LORD. He that sweareth to [his own] hurt, and changeth not. [He that] putteth not out his money to usury, nor taketh reward against the innocent. He that doeth these [things] shall never be moved.
>
> (Ps. 15:1-5)

God says we must walk uprightly. This does not mean that we must attain absolute moral perfection. Rather, it means that we must have a strong heartfelt desire to love and serve God and walk in a right way as best we can. Those who "worketh righteousness" practice justice, fairness, and forgiveness. Those who "speaketh the truth" declare the gospel truth without compromise. These people give highest priority to seek God's purposes and the rule of His kingdom.

> Who shall ascend into the hill of the LORD? or who shall stand in his holy place? He that hath clean hands, and a pure heart; who hath not lifted up his soul unto vanity, nor sworn deceitfully. He shall receive the blessing from the LORD, and righteousness from the God of his salvation.
>
> (Ps. 24:3-5)

We have clean hands when we live in such a way as to not defile ourselves with worldly enticements. We have a pure heart when we desire to live righteously and seek purity and holiness before the Lord. The Lord knows we will stumble, but He is more concerned about our heart attitude (see 1 Samuel 16:7). If we desire to do right and fail, that is entirely different from desiring to do wrong and succeeding. Our motives and the attitude of our heart are extremely important to the Lord. An outward appearance of righteousness does not necessarily mean that we are inwardly righteous in God's sight.

> For I say unto you, That except your righteousness shall exceed [the righteousness] of the scribes and Pharisees, ye shall in no case enter into the kingdom of heaven.
>
> (Matt. 5:20)

The word "exceed" means extreme abundance or excess. The Pharisees appeared to be the most righteous in keeping the Law. The scribes copied the Word without error. Both groups considered themselves to be perfect keepers of the Law and above reproach. Yet Jesus told the Pharisees and the scribes that no matter how good *they* thought they were, they would not enter the Kingdom because their assumed righteousness was not adequate.

> But we are all as an [unclean thing], and all our righteous-nesses [are] as filthy rags; and we all do fade as a leaf; and our iniquities, like the wind, have taken us away.
>
> (Isa. 64:6)

Assumed righteousness is like appearing before God in defiled garments. God views our attempts to establish our own righteousness as detestable.

> As it is written, There is none righteous, no, not one.
>
> (Rom. 3:10)

We are all in the same condition. In God's sight we are all unrighteous until He imputes the righteousness of Jesus to us.

> And he showed me Joshua the high priest standing before the angel of the LORD, and Satan standing at his right hand to resist (accuse) him. And the LORD said unto Satan, The LORD rebuke thee, O Satan; even the LORD that hath cho-sen Jerusalem rebuke thee: [is] not this a brand plucked out of the fire? Now Joshua was clothed with filthy garments, and stood before the angel. And he answered and spake unto those that stood before him, saying, Take away the filthy gar-ments from him. And unto him he said, Behold, I have caused thine iniquity to pass from thee, and I will clothe thee with change of raiment.
>
> (Zech. 3:1-4)

In this passage, Zechariah saw Joshua, the high priest and supposedly the most holy and righteous man in Israel, stand-ing before the Lord clothed in filthy garments. Then God took away the filthy garments and replaced them with clean clothes, signifying his redemption. Joshua only had to be willing. Note that the clean garments were not put over the filthy ones—the new garments *replaced* the filthy garments.

> And to her was granted that she should be arrayed in fine linen, clean and white: for the fine linen is the righteousness of saints.
>
> (Rev. 19:8)

Fine linen is symbolic of the righteous *acts* of the saints (*NIV*). The works we accomplish in the way that God asks us to accomplish them count as righteousness to us. As James notes, "Abraham believed God, and it was imputed unto him for righteousness" (2:23).

In the parable of the wedding (see Matthew 22:11-13), everyone wore a wedding garment except one man. When the king saw this man's attire, he instructed his servants to bind him and throw him into the outer darkness because he wasn't properly clothed. In other words, this man had not worked out and walked out righteousness. "He that doeth righteousness is righteous, even as he is righteous" (1 John 3:7).

> For if by one man's offence death reigned by one; much more they which receive abundance of grace and of the gift of righteousness shall reign in life by one, Jesus Christ.
>
> (Rom. 5:17)

We cannot earn righteousness. We can't buy it. We don't deserve it. We only receive it through the substitution at the cross in which Jesus bore our sin. Righteousness is a gift.

It is said that there is no testimony without a test. Every choice is a test that reveals our inner motives and attitudes as to whether we will do what honors God (righteousness) or what pleases ourselves.

When I worked in a machine tool factory, I would get coffee from a vending machine several times a day. As all mechanical devices do, the coffee machine often malfunctioned. Whenever the machine failed, I reported the problem to the personnel department, and they refunded my money.

One day, the machine dispensed the coffee *and* returned the money I had put in. This presented me with a dilemma: would I consider myself fortunate for having received something for nothing, or would I make a different choice? By the grace of God, I was able to recognize the situation as a test. I decided to do what was righteous. When I went to the personnel department and gave back the money, the person who received it was astonished. This provided me with the opportunity to say, "When one decides to follow Jesus, He influences us to want to do what is right."

We cannot understand righteousness without considering unrighteousness. The most frequent expression of unrighteousness among Christians is that of judging and criticizing others. The sin of self-righteousness is often the source of a judgmental and critical attitude. Speaking evil of another person is the same as judging them (see James 4:11). Pride is closely associated with self-righteousness and expresses itself by exalting self or by demeaning others.

> Looking diligently lest any man fail of the grace of God; lest any root of bitterness springing up trouble you, and thereby many be defiled.
>
> (Heb. 12:15)

We "fail of grace" as a result of our pride expressed as self-righteousness. If we persist in being critical or judgmental, we develop what the Bible calls a "root of bitterness." Peter states, "God resisteth the proud and giveth grace to the humble" (1 Peter 5:5). Self-righteousness mars our relationship with God and strains our relationships with others. It can also have a detrimental effect on our physical bodies.

Our judgment may bind people in the behavior that troubles us. It is even possible that we can bind their sin to ourselves. When this occurs, we then exhibit the same behavior we dislike in them. If we find character defects we dislike in others manifesting in our lives, unrighteous judgment of others may be the cause.

A judgment must pass three tests to determine whether it is righteous or unrighteous. The first test is *whether we have the God-given authority to judge.* Is what we are about to judge in another person under the authority God has given us, or are we acting presumptuously?

The second test is *the standard of comparison*. In John 12:47-48, Jesus tells us He didn't come to judge the world but to save it. Jesus said His Word would judge each of us in the last day. The standard of comparison in righteous judgment is the Word of God. Righteous judgment will not be based on our likes, dislikes or opinions.

The third test is *the reason for making a judgment at this time*. If we judge on what we see or hear apart from the revelation of God, we are likely to make an unrighteous judgment. Unless the Lord reveals something to us, the matter will largely be unknown to us. We should thus judge only when we receive instruction (a *rhema* word) from God.

> And he spake this parable unto certain which trusted in themselves that they were righteous, and despised others: Two men went up into the temple to pray; the one a Pharisee, and the other a publican. The Pharisee stood and prayed thus with himself, God, I thank thee, that I am not as other men are, extortioners, unjust, adulterers, or even as this publican. I fast twice in the week, I give tithes of all that I possess. And the publican, standing afar off, would not lift up so much as his eyes unto heaven, but smote upon his breast, saying, God be merciful to me a sinner. I tell you, this man went down to his house justified rather than the other: for every one that exalteth himself shall be abased; and he that humbleth himself shall be exalted.
>
> (Luke 18:9-14)

The Pharisee is a perfect example of one who exhibited self-righteousness and lifted himself above others. Such self-righteousness can be manifested in criticizing, accusing, and finding fault in others. It seeks to knock other people far enough down so that we will look good by comparison. If we want to be righteous, we will compare ourselves only to Jesus. If you find judging, accusing, criticizing, and faultfinding words coming out

of your mouth, please entreat the Holy Spirit to bring conviction—and then come quickly to repentance.

> And why beholdest thou the mote that is in thy brother's eye,
> but considerest not the beam that is in thine own eye? Or
> how wilt thou say to thy brother, Let me pull out the mote
> out of thine eye; and, behold, a beam is in thine own eye?
> Thou hypocrite, first cast out the beam out of thine own eye;
> and then shalt thou see clearly to cast out the mote out of thy
> brother's eye.
>
> (Matt. 7:3-5)

A "mote," according to Thayer's Lexicon, is a tiny piece of
straw or chaff. A "beam" is a huge timber capable of supporting
a heavy weight. Jesus was saying that the same fault we see and
judge in another person is *much worse* in us.

> For they being ignorant of God's righteousness, and going
> about to establish their own righteousness, have not submit-
> ted themselves unto the righteousness of God. For Christ is
> the end of the law for righteousness to every one that be-
> lieveth. For Moses describeth the righteousness which is of
> the law, That the man which doeth those things shall live by
> them.
>
> (Rom. 10:3-5)

To try and establish our righteousness is an act of ignorance.
Christ is the end of the law of righteousness by works.

> Judge not, that ye be not judged. For with what judgment ye
> judge, ye shall be judged: and with what measure ye mete, it
> shall be measured to you again.
>
> (Matt. 7:1-2)

Some people can really irritate us and get under our skin the
instant we are with them. Suddenly, we find ourselves reacting
and becoming offended. However, if we demand perfect behavior
from others, God will require the same from us. God is going to

measure back to us what we have measured out to others. He will hold us to the same standard by which we measure others.

> Therefore, thou art inexcusable, O man, whosoever thou art that judgest: for Where in thou judgest another, thou condemnest thyself; for thou that judgest doest the same things.
>
> (Rom. 2:1)

The Greek word for "condemn" in this verse is *katakrino*, which means to judge against or to pass sentence. *Kata* is the emphatic prefix that means intensity, which is *strong* judgment. If someone irritates us, what we really have is a spiritual mirror reflecting back on us. What we are feeling is our own condemnation from judgment coming back on us because we have unrighteously judged the person who is irritating us. It has been said that if someone is "getting our goat," it only proves that we have a goat to get!

God once demonstrated this principle to my wife and me. Every time I drove a particular road, I hit a pothole. For weeks, the highway workers never fixed that hole. Every time I drove down that road, I hit the pothole, and every time I hit the pothole, my wife would get on my case. She would ask what in the world was the matter with me. Why couldn't I remember that hole was there? Was I spaced out or something? Wasn't I conscious of what was going on? She became more and more upset each time I continued to hit the pothole.

I became more and more perplexed. It wasn't so much that I was troubled as that I was frustrated. Why couldn't I remember that pothole? Whenever I drove down that road with her in the car, miles ahead of that pothole I would ask God to remind me of it so that I wouldn't hit it. That didn't work. I would come around the corner, down the hill, and hit that pothole again.

One day, we were again approaching that place in the road. I did not pray, but as I drove I heard the Spirit speak to me and say, "Move over to the left a little bit. You will miss the hole." I moved over to the left, went around the corner, down the hill, and missed the pothole. My wife looked at me and asked, "Do you want to go back and try again?"

I told my wife that I didn't know why God hadn't answered in the past when I asked Him to remind me of that hole but had spoken this time. She replied rather quietly, "Maybe something changed." I asked what she meant. She said, "Well, today I let go of it and said, 'God if he hits the hole, he hits the hole. It's Your problem.'"

We learned that day that when we hold people in judgment, they will continue the negative behavior until we let go of the judgment. If we have people in our lives that are bothering us and their behavior doesn't seem to be improving, maybe *we* are the problem.

This principle is clearly stated in John 20:23: "Whose soever sins ye remit, they are remitted unto them; and whose soever sins ye retain, they are retained." If we unrighteously judge people, we retain their sins. They will continue hitting that bump in our lives, aggravating us and destroying our peace and joy. When we stop judging, God will change their behavior. Ironically, it happened that several days later when my wife was driving down that road, she hit the pothole. I had nothing to say.

> But we are all as an unclean thing, *and all our righteousnesses are as filthy rags;* and we all do fade as a leaf; and our iniquities, like the wind, have taken us away.
>
> (Isa. 64:6, emphasis added)

Self-righteousness is an ugly sin because it essentially negates the work of the cross. It is an attitude that says, "I am righteous in my own right. I don't need the righteousness of Jesus." No wonder God so strongly opposes it. We need to ask the Holy Spirit for revelation and deep conviction of any sins of unrighteous judgments, pride, and self-righteousness in our lives and then ask for forgiveness for those specific sins.

> Being filled with the fruits of righteousness, which are by Jesus Christ, unto the glory and praise of God.
>
> (Phil. 1:11)

If we are filled with the fruits of righteousness, which result from living in the Spirit, we will bring glory and praise to God. People who don't know God will notice that our lives are different. They will see the good we do and find that we live above reproach. They will have no basis to find fault in us.

> For ye were sometimes darkness, but now are ye light in the Lord: walk as children of light: (For the fruit of the Spirit is in all goodness and righteousness and truth;) Proving what is acceptable unto the Lord.
>
> (Eph. 5:8-10)

If we walk in righteousness, we will not harm anyone. We will treat everyone with respect and kindness. We will exhibit righteousness as we relate to others.

> Little children, let no man deceive you: he that doeth righteousness is righteous, even as he is righteous. He that committeth sin is of the devil; for the devil sinneth from the beginning. For this purpose the Son of God was manifested, that he might destroy the works of the devil. Whosoever is born of God doth not commit sin; for his seed remaineth in him: and he cannot sin, because he is born of God. In this the children of God are manifest, and the children of the devil: *whosoever doeth not righteousness is not of God*, neither he that loveth not his brother.
>
> (1 John 3 7-10, emphasis added)

Righteous living proves righteousness. Those who commit willful sins without repentance will not inherit the kingdom of God (see 1 Corinthians 6:9-10). This does not refer to people who sin out of ignorance or who simply make a mistake, but rather those who don't care about how they live. These individuals are lawless and independent. They may think they are righteous, but their lives will prove otherwise.

> He that followeth after righteousness and mercy findeth life, righteousness and honor.
>
> (Prov. 21:21)

If we seek righteousness, we will follow Jesus. If we follow Jesus, we will become like Him. The life of Jesus will express itself through us and replace our self-life.

> And if Christ [be] in you, the body [is] dead because of sin; but the Spirit [is] life because of righteousness.
>
> (Rom. 8:10)

We have been born-again with seed incorruptible (see 1 Peter 1:23) and can request God to reveal this new nature within us. We can simply pray, "God, I want Your seed to replace my old genetics. I want to do what comes naturally to the new nature, not the old nature. God, because You are in me, I'm able to do what you want if I simply choose to do it" (see Philippians 4:13).

Of course, we have some responsibility in this. Everything we need to realize this new nature has been provided to us except one: a willingness to use what we have been given. If we use what the Lord has given us to the best of our ability—even if imperfectly—we are considered righteous. "For the LORD seeth not as man seeth; for man looketh on the outward appearance, but the LORD looketh on the heart" (1 Samuel 16:7). God looks more at our internals (motives and attitudes) than He does at our externals.

> Thou lovest righteousness, and hatest wickedness: therefore God, thy God, hath anointed thee with the oil of gladness above thy fellows.
>
> (Ps. 45:7)

If we love righteousness and hate wickedness, we can walk with confidence that God is pleased regardless of our circumstances. God's righteousness is a manifestation of His nature, which is to be merciful and giving. When He brings His nature of love and mercy to us, He is expressing who He is to us. When we express His nature to others, we are revealing God.

> For he put on righteousness as a breastplate, and an helmet of salvation upon his head; and he put on the garments of vengeance [for] clothing, and was clad with zeal as a cloak.
>
> (Isa. 59:17)

> Stand therefore, having your loins girt about with truth, and having on the breastplate of righteousness.
>
> (Eph. 6:14)

God's righteousness—not our own—is a spiritual breastplate that we should wear. A breastplate protects the upper torso, which is a way of saying that we are to guard our heart. Righteous acts are thus the outward expression of the inward attitudes and motives of our heart.

> What then? Israel hath not obtained that which he seeketh for; but the election hath obtained it, and the rest were *blinded* (According as it is written, God hath given them the spirit of slumber, eyes that they should not see, and ears that they should not hear;) unto this day.
>
> (Rom. 11:7-8, (emphasis added)

Another translation for the word "blinded" is "hardened." Becoming hardened is the result of habitually resisting the will of God and demanding that we have our own way. It is a stubborn, unyielding attitude that leads to a hardening of our hearts. Pharaoh's heart was hardened because he resisted God again and again. Defeat and destruction came to him as a result.

> Awake to righteousness, and sin not; for some have not the knowledge of God: I speak [this] to your shame.
>
> (1 Cor. 15:34)

If we are called to wake up to righteousness, it means we have been asleep! The idea of waking out of a slumber is similar to shaking off self-deception. Scripture implies that those who know what they should be doing but don't do it are acting in an unrighteous manner (see James 4:17). This also applies to people who know that God has given them a task but neglect to do it or do it incompletely.

> And Jesus answering said unto him [John the Baptist], Suffer [it to be so] now: for thus it becometh us to fulfill all righteousness. Then he suffered him.
>
> (Matt. 3:15)

I believe Jesus could have said something like, "John, we've got to do what the Father wants. Even though you and I are different, we have to do it because God wants it done." Sometimes, the only reason we will ever get from God for doing something is simply that He wants it done. God is not obligated to explain Himself.

We are not called to decide what we should and shouldn't do. That would be living out of the Tree of the Knowledge of Good and Evil. As Rick Joyner teaches, the good side of this tree is just as toxic as the evil side, because it represents living by our own strength and wisdom instead of trusting the Lord.

When Jesus said, "Seek ye first the Kingdom of God and His righteousness" (Matthew 6:33), He meant that we seek to have God rule us, not just guide us or supply our needs. We must seek how God wants us to live and behave—His way, not our way. To God, it is more important that we be righteous than be "right." He may, if He chooses, ask us to apologize for a wrong perceived by someone, even if He knows that we did nothing wrong. God wants peace—not strife—in His house.

> For the kingdom of God is not meat and drink; but righteousness, and peace, and joy in the Holy Ghost. For he that in these things serveth Christ [is] acceptable to God, and approved of men. Let us therefore follow after the things which make for peace, and things wherewith one may edify another.
>
> (Rom. 14:17-19)

If we live according to the principles of God's kingdom, we will express the virtues of righteousness, peace and joy. The opposing kingdom manifests competition, strife and despair. We need to occasionally do a reality check on ourselves to see which kingdom principles we exhibit. Righteous living is proof of our commitment to the Lord.

Chapter 7

COMMITMENT

Do you have a cost you are unwilling to meet? A price you will not pay? A place you will not go? A work you will not do for God? Have you knowingly or unknowingly drawn a boundary you will not cross?

Webster's Dictionary defines "commitment" as a pledge or a promise. It is derived from a compound Latin word consisting of *com*, which means together, and *mittere*, which means to send. Commitment thus means to be sent together. Christians are brought together by God's initiative and then are sent together to do His will (see 1 Corinthians 12:18). God brings us together, but we must respond with our personal commitment.

> And he answering said, Thou shalt love the Lord thy God with all thy heart, and with all thy soul, and with all thy strength, and with all thy mind; and thy neighbor as thyself.
>
> (Luke 10:27)

The commandment is to love the Lord with all our heart, soul, strength and mind. This leaves nothing out. Clearly, all that we are and everything we have is to be committed to love the Lord.

> Wherefore the Lord said, Forasmuch as this people draw near [me] with their mouth, and with their lips do honor me, but

have removed their heart far from me, and their fear toward me is taught by the precept of men: Therefore, behold, I will proceed to do a marvelous work among this people, [even] a marvelous work and a wonder: for the wisdom of their wise [men] shall perish, and the understanding of their prudent [men] shall be hid.

(Isa. 29:13-14)

In this passage, the Lord was speaking about the tendency of people to make religion a tradition. Religion without relationship is not pleasing to God, and He will move strongly against such pretense. He will confound all those who consider themselves wise. Serving God with our lips alone is not enough; we must serve Him with our hearts.

God once convicted me of mindless rote religion as I was reciting the Lord's Prayer as a part of a church service. As I said the prayer, the Lord asked me what I thought I was doing. I realized that while I was reciting the prayer, I was thinking about several projects at home that needed to be done after church. It was an empty religious act because neither my mind nor my heart was involved.

Therefore thus saith the Lord GOD, Behold, I lay in Zion for a foundation a stone, a tried stone, a precious corner [stone], a sure foundation: he that believeth shall not make haste.

(Isa. 28:16)

The Lord Jesus Christ must be the cornerstone of our lives. He is the rock, the cornerstone and the point of reference that has everything to do with our lives. If our foundation is not built on the cornerstone that is Jesus, we will not have stability or move in the correct direction. Our lives will be out of line and off balance. If we place our security in our homes, possessions, parents, church, or friends, we will discover that these do not bring security. If our security is not in God, we will have no true security.

A cornerstone is level, plumb and square. It establishes the three perfect planes of reference by which a building is constructed. In the same way, the Lord Jesus is our constant reference point. We must go to that single point of reference for everything we do in our lives. We must not take our reference from what other people are doing, or what we think or feel, or even what we hope to accomplish. Only when we take our reference back to the Lord Jesus, to the Word of God, to the cornerstone of our lives, will we have true security and be aligned with the purposes of God. We must be *committed to an unrelenting progression.* Comfort and contentment with immaturity must be unacceptable to us.

> Then said he, Lo, I come to do thy will, O God. He taketh away the first, that he may establish the second.
>
> (Heb. 10:9)

The words "taketh away" mean to put away and abolish with the implication of finality. God will abolish things in our lives that we think are good. He will abolish contentment with the status quo, our familiar surroundings, and our worldly reputation. If we rest, trust, or base our lives in these things, we are on shifting sand. They have no strength, no stability, and will not support us. God has to take away some of the things we think are good so that He can establish better things.

> Take you twelve men out of the people, out of every tribe a man, And command ye them, saying, Take you hence out of the midst of Jordan, out of the place where the priests' feet stood firm, twelve stones, and ye shall carry them over with you, and leave them in the lodging place, *where ye shall lodge this night.*
>
> (Josh. 4:2-3, emphasis added)

God did not intend the Israelites to cross over the Jordan into the Promised Land, build a memorial, and then sit on it while looking back across the river, saying, "Wasn't it wonderful when God divided the water?" Many believers do exactly this—they live in their memories of what God did instead of looking forward to what He has promised.

We must get off our memorial stones. God expects us to press on into the Land of Promise and take the whole of our inheritance. We should not sit down and look back, saying, "Wasn't it nice when..." Carnal contentment in what we have gained spiritually diminishes our zeal for continuing on to gain more. God will confront any attitude of contentment in us that inhibits progress.

> Not as though I had already attained, either were already perfect: but I follow after, if that I may apprehend that for which also I am apprehended of Christ Jesus. Brethren, I count not myself to have apprehended: but [this] one thing [I do], forgetting those things which are behind, and reaching forth unto those things which are before, I press toward the mark for the prize of the high calling of God in Christ Jesus.
>
> (Phil. 3:12-14)

The phrase "I follow after" means to ardently pursue or strongly seek after. It is not wishful thinking; it is a committed and persistent course of action. We must let go of what is behind us and make a strong effort to advance.

When our boys were small, we had a summer cottage with a small dock on a lake. The boys would wear their swimsuits under their clothes, and when we got to the cottage, they would fly out of the car leaving a trail of T-shirts, sneakers and socks all the way to the dock. They would run to the end of the dock and launch themselves into the air. I would yell, "Stop!" But obviously, they couldn't stop; they were committed.

We must be settled and grounded in Jesus. Like Joshua, who left nothing undone that God required of him (see Joshua 11:15), we must be committed to become all that God intends. He has committed Himself to finish the good work that He has started in us (see Philippians 1:6).

> Therefore leaving the principles of the doctrine of Christ, let us go on unto perfection; not laying again the foundation of repentance from dead works, and of faith toward God, Of the

doctrine of baptisms, and of laying on of hands, and of resurrection of the dead, and of eternal judgment.

(Heb. 6: 1-2)

The word "perfection" can be understood to mean maturity and completeness. We should not be satisfied to gain half of the Promised Land and then say, "Well, let's stop here." This is not the right mindset. The words "go on" in this passage, according to *Thayer's Lexicon*, mean to be moved inwardly. The determination must be created and applied from within. We shouldn't have to be goaded onward. The impetus to go on must be part of our inmost being.

Additionally, "go on" means "to be prompted by the application of force or pressure." It is like the action of wind in a sail. The sail catches the wind, which moves the boat. The wind in our sails is the power of the Holy Spirit. We must allow the pressure of His flow to move us forward in the kingdom of God.

> But, beloved, we are persuaded better things of you, and things that accompany salvation, though we thus speak. For God [is] not unrighteous to forget your work and labor of love, which ye have shown toward his name, in that ye have ministered to the saints, and do minister. And we desire that every one of you do show the same diligence to the full assurance of hope unto the end: That ye be not slothful, but followers of them who *through faith and patience* inherit the promises.
>
> (Heb. 6:9-12, emphasis added)

We must be diligent and not lazy! We must continue to move ahead to inherit the promises of God. Note that *both* faith and patience are required.

> And from the days of John the Baptist until now the kingdom of heaven suffereth violence, and the violent take it by force.
>
> (Matt. 11:12)

Taking the Kingdom by force expresses the idea of running full speed toward an obstacle and then throwing all of our being against it in a violent effort to dislodge it. It is an absolute commitment to use everything we are and everything we have to overcome.

Some time ago, the Lord gave me a dream about a great battle. In the dream, I could see the cross of Jesus in the distance silhouetted against fiery artillery bursts. I knew that I was viewing a spiritual battle and that I had been called of the Lord to participate in the conflict. As dawn broke, I saw a road winding from the cross through the hills to the battle, where I was standing. A massive roadblock teeming with heavily armed enemy soldiers cut off the road. I yearned to be in the battle, where I knew God wanted me to be, but I knew that I couldn't get to the fight with that obstacle blocking my path. Then a hand came down from heaven and swept away the obstacle. The way was open, and I went forward to join the battle.

Through the dream, God showed me that He would remove the obstacles, but He expected me to change my mind about something in my life. At the time, I was consuming a substantial amount of alcohol every weekend. The dream clearly related to that issue. God would remove the obstacle, but I had to take action and desire to go forward. I could not stay where I was and be content, for that obstacle in my life would prevent me from going deeper into God.

This interpretation was confirmed later that morning when I heard the guest speaker on a Christian TV program interrupt his message and say, "Someone out there has an obstacle between himself and the cross, and God wants it dealt with now." We all have obstacles that prevent us from becoming all that God wants us to be. We need to pray to God that He will reveal those obstacles and then show us how to remove them. We are accountable to God to be *committed to what has been entrusted to us in an uncompromising way.*

> As we said before, so say I now again, If any [man] preach any other gospel unto you than that ye have received, let him be accursed.
>
> (Gal. 1:9)

We can never allow any other gospel, social or otherwise, to be substituted for the pure gospel of the New Testament that was written under the anointed direction of the Holy Spirit. We must not compromise what has been entrusted to us.

We should thus be wary if someone comes to us or to our home, as some cult members do, and preaches another gospel. They may preach another Jesus who is not one of the personalities of the Triune God. If they declare that there is no Satan or hell, or if they preach a social action gospel instead of repentance of sin, we must not receive them (see 2 John 1:10). These individuals are preaching a gospel contrary to Scripture. Because they spread error, false teaching and deception, they bring a curse on themselves. Sins of ignorance are still sins.

> That we [henceforth] be no more children, tossed to and fro, and carried about with every wind of doctrine, by the sleight of men, [and] cunning craftiness, whereby they lie in wait to deceive.
>
> (Eph. 4:14)

Some people preach the gospel with the wrong motives. These false teachers continually create new ways to merchandise their ministry and cause some Christians to be carried about. These immature believers move through doubt and hesitation from one opinion to the next, focusing on one thing and then another, or going from one doctrine to another. These believers are never settled or secure in their faith. They continually chase the popular message of the day and never build a firm faith foundation.

Some Christians focus too much on end-times teachings. They lose their focus on the preeminent purpose of God, which is for us to be transformed into the likeness of Jesus. We must keep our eyes on the ultimate prize that is Christ.

A "religious" believer once asked me, "Brother, do you keep the Sabbath?" I knew where he was going and I had no desire to get into an argument. So I replied, "Yes, I do, all seven of them." This answer left him speechless. Focusing too much on these doctrines, even though they contain truth, distracts us from the central truth of Christianity.

> For though I be absent in the flesh, yet I am with you in the spirit, joying and beholding your order, and the steadfastness of your faith in Christ. As ye have therefore received Christ Jesus the Lord, [so] walk ye in him; Rooted and built up in him, and stablished in the faith, as ye have been taught, abounding therein with thanksgiving. Beware lest any man spoil you through philosophy and vain deceit, after the tradition of men, after the rudiments of the world, and not after Christ.
>
> (Col. 2:5-8)

The Word instructs us to not let traditions or worldly wisdom take us away from the centrality of Jesus. We shouldn't let compromise or distraction influence the life He has given us.

> Let no man beguile you of your reward in a voluntary humility and worshipping of angels, intruding into those things which he hath not seen, vainly puffed up by his fleshly mind, And not holding the Head, from which all the body by joints and bands having nourishment ministered, and knit together, increaseth with the increase of God.
>
> (Col. 2:18-19)

We "increase" by holding fast to the Head, which is the Lord Jesus, and by maintaining an intimate relationship with Him. If we do this, we won't be drawn into substituting another doctrine for the gospel truth.

> Thus saith the LORD; Cursed [be] the man that trusteth in man, and maketh flesh his arm, and whose heart departeth from the LORD. For he shall be like the heath in the desert, and shall not see when good cometh; but shall inhabit the parched places in the wilderness, [in] a salt land and not inhabited. Blessed [is] the man that trusteth in the LORD, and whose hope the LORD is. For he shall be as a tree planted by the waters, and [that] spreadeth out her roots by the river,

and shall not see when heat cometh, but her leaf shall be green; and shall not be careful in the year of drought, neither shall cease from yielding fruit.

(Jer. 17:5-8)

Actions have consequences. If we live in our carnal nature and put our trust in people, human wisdom, or our abilities, God says we will experience spiritual drought. However, if we put our trust, hope, confidence and commitment in God, we will be abundantly blessed. In time of need, I believe we should go to the throne before we go to the phone. If the One on the throne then tells us to go to the phone, we can call others in faith and obedience to seek help.

He will not suffer thy foot to be moved; he that keepeth thee will not slumber.

(Ps. 121:3)

If we stand where God has placed us, He won't allow our foot to be moved. However, if we wander around seeking things other than God's will, we will encounter problems. We could find ourselves in spiritual quicksand.

I read a story written by an excellent Christian author named Jamie Buckingham in which he told of a vision he received during his early years as a Christian. In this vision, he saw himself with a group moving through the wilderness on new paths. Occasionally, he would leave the group God had set him in and go off exploring on his own to see what was over the next hill. When he did so, he would see himself returning bloodied and bruised, black-eyed and limping, with his clothes tattered and torn and yelling at the top of his lungs, "NOT THAT WAY! NOT THAT WAY!" He said he experienced this vision a few times until he finally got the message that he would get into trouble if he didn't stay where God had placed him or go where God had sent him.

For they loved the praise of men more than the praise of God.

(John 12:43)

In this verse, John is describing the Jewish priests who believed in Jesus but remained connected to the old order. They would not make a public commitment and confession of the Lord Jesus because they were afraid they would be thrown out of the synagogue. They regarded their reputation and position as more valuable than their personal identification with the Lord Jesus. May God call us to repentance if we do that! If we set anything—even our affiliation with a particular church—above our commitment to Him, it is idolatry.

> The fear of man bringeth a snare: but whoso putteth his trust in the Lord shall be safe.
>
> (Prov. 29:25)

A "snare" is a trap. We can become trapped by fear of what people might think of us so that we are unable to progress in God's kingdom. Ultimately, only the praise we receive from God is truly meaningful and eternal. We cannot keep our commitment if we can't move forward. We must be *committed to the truth.*

> Go and proclaim these words toward the north, and say, Return, thou backsliding Israel, saith the LORD; [and] I will not cause mine anger to fall upon you: for I [am] merciful, saith the LORD, [and] I will not keep [anger] for ever. Only acknowledge thine iniquity, that thou hast transgressed against the LORD thy God, and hast scattered thy ways to the strangers under every green tree, and ye have not obeyed my voice, saith the LORD. Turn, O backsliding children, saith the LORD; for I am married unto you: and I will take you one of a city, and two of a family, and I will bring you to Zion.
>
> (Jer. 3:12-14)

God says we must acknowledge our backsliding and the fact that we have sinned. We must be willing to admit that we have failed, are headed the wrong way, or have a wrong idea. When we are willing to admit our faults, turn around, and return to righteousness, God promises restoration. He says He will receive us.

The story of the prodigal son is God's promise that He will always welcome returning repentant sinners without condemnation.

My wife bought a picture of two little pigs, one facing one way and one facing the other. The caption under the picture said, "If you find yourself headed in the wrong direction, remember, God allows U-turns."

> Be not deceived; God is not mocked: for whatsoever a man soweth, that shall he also reap. For he that soweth to his flesh shall of the flesh reap corruption; but he that soweth to the Spirit shall of the Spirit reap life everlasting. And let us not be weary in well doing: for in due season we shall reap, if we faint not.
>
> (Gal. 6:7-9)

If we move away from the rule of the Spirit, our flesh (self-lives) will produce corruption. We must never cease trying to live a godly life or slip into apathy or passivity. God calls us to a progressive walk. We cannot waver or let opposition exhaust us so that we become too tired to press on. If opposition increases against us, we must just push harder. We can't back off or give up.

> And Ruth said, Entreat me not to leave thee, [or] to return from following after thee: for whither thou goest, I will go; and where thou lodgest, I will lodge: thy people [shall] be my people, and thy God my God: Where thou diest, will I die, and there I will be buried: the LORD do so to me, and more also, [if aught] but death part thee and me. When she saw that she was steadfastly minded to go with her, then she left speaking unto her.
>
> (Ruth 1:16-18)

To be "steadfastly minded" means to have a settled, determined and unwavering mind. Our confession should be like that of Ruth: "Where You go, I will follow." We may not know where we are going, but we know Who we are following—and that must be enough. Otherwise, we will be governed by our intellect rather than by the Spirit.

> Prove all things; hold fast that which is good.
>
> (1 Thess. 5:21)

The phrase "hold fast" means to keep in memory, to possess and seize upon, or to be unwavering.

> For we are made partakers of Christ, if we hold the beginning of our confidence steadfast unto the end.
>
> (Heb. 3:14)

The word "partakers" means to be a participant, a sharer and a partner. It means to be joined together for a common purpose. If we are to benefit from this partnership, we must be persistent and "steadfast"—solid, stable, strong, unmovable, firm, and sure settled in our mind.

> Let us hold fast the profession of [our] faith without wavering; (for he is faithful that promised).
>
> (Heb. 10:23)

If we choose to hold on, God will give us the strength we need. The word "profession" refers to a covenant or an acknowledgement. We must hold securely the profession of our faith, the confession of our belief, and be *committed to an immovable decision.*

> Be sober, be vigilant; because your adversary the devil, as a roaring lion, walketh about, seeking whom he may devour: Whom resist steadfast in the faith, knowing that the same afflictions are accomplished in your brethren that are in the world. But the God of all grace, who hath called us unto his eternal glory by Christ Jesus, after that ye have suffered a while, make you perfect, stablish, strengthen, settle [you].
>
> (1 Pet. 5:8-10)

We are called to be active and determined in resisting Satan and steadfast in our faith. When we are vigilant and steadfast, God promises that He will make us "perfect," which means to mend that which is broken; "stablish," which means to make as solid as granite; "strengthen," which means to be filled with strength; and "settled," which means to lay the foundation. God will do this for us if we make up our minds to do our part. Our part is to submit to God, resist the Devil and be immovable in faith (see James 4:7). We must decide to say, "God, I'm going on with You no matter what."

> And now, behold, I go bound in the spirit unto Jerusalem, not knowing the things that shall befall me there: Save that the Holy Ghost witnesseth in every city, saying that bonds and afflictions abide me. But none of these things move me, neither count I my life dear unto myself, so that I might finish my course with joy, and the ministry, which I have received of the Lord Jesus, to testify the gospel of the grace of God.
> (Acts 20:22-24)

When Paul was preparing to be taken into Jerusalem, he didn't know what he would encounter. He knew that the Spirit had repeatedly told him that he was headed for prison and trouble. But in effect, he said, "so what!"

> Therefore, my beloved brethren, be ye steadfast, unmovable, always abounding in the work of the Lord, forasmuch as ye know that your labor is not in vain in the Lord.
> (1 Cor. 15:58)

"Abounding" means to excel and be superior. If we do something half-heartedly, the result will be unpleasing to God. We must not be passive but active. We must not be ruled by our carnal nature but governed by the Spirit.

> But call to remembrance the former days, in which, after ye were illuminated, ye endured a great fight of afflictions;
> Partly, whilst ye were made a gazingstock both by reproaches

and afflictions; and partly, whilst ye became companions of them that were so used. For ye had compassion of me in my bonds, and took joyfully the spoiling of your goods, knowing in yourselves that ye have in heaven a better and an enduring substance. Cast not away therefore your confidence, which hath great recompense of reward. For ye have need of patience, that, after ye have done the will of God, ye might receive the promise.

(Heb. 10:32-36)

We must endure afflictions, be confident, do the will of God and not draw back. We must stay on course despite the adverse circumstances we may encounter.

Wherefore the rather, brethren, give diligence to make your calling and election sure: for if ye do these things, ye shall never fall.

(2 Pet. 1:10)

We must not compromise what God has given but cling to it with firmness and purity. We must commit to having a determined mind and be firm in our decision that the Lord will be the most, the singular, the highest, and the central focus of our lives. We must commit to an immovable decision that troubles, disappointments, trials, and circumstances that don't work out our way will not move us off course. We must tell ourselves that even when we run into hard times, we will not draw back but push harder. That is commitment! That will enable us to consistently honor and express our covenant with God.

Chapter 8

COVENANT

Can you accurately describe and fully explain what a covenant is? Do you comprehend the benefits and demands of covenant living with God? With one another? If you do, are you living what you believe?

Covenant is the joining together of two parties and requires a full and strong commitment. A covenant is of the spirit, whereas a contract is of the flesh (world system). A contract is weak and often broken, but a covenant remains binding even if one party does not honor it. God initiates covenant with His people. He neither debates nor negotiates. We enter into covenant with God only on His terms and conditions. Covenants are intended to be forever. God's covenants are irrevocable.

> *But with thee will I establish my covenant*; and thou shalt come into the ark, thou, and thy sons, and thy wife, and thy sons' wives with thee.
>
> (Gen. 6:18, emphasis added)

God made a covenant with Noah for his deliverance and safety. God sealed Noah and his family in the ark and saved them from the flood. The covenant with Noah foreshadows the New Testament experience of a believer. Jesus is our ark of safety and our deliverance from the storm.

And the bow shall be in the cloud; and I will look upon it, that I may remember the everlasting covenant between God and every living creature of all flesh that [is] upon the earth.

(Gen. 9:16)

The rainbow is a covenant sign for all living creatures that God will never again use a worldwide flood to destroy life on earth.

And when Abram was ninety years old and nine, the LORD appeared to Abram, and said unto him, I [am] the Almighty God; walk before me, and be thou perfect. *And I will make my covenant between me and thee*, and will multiply thee exceedingly. And Abram fell on his face: and God talked with him, saying, As for me, behold, my covenant [is] with thee, and thou shalt be a father of many nations. Neither shall thy name any more be called Abram, but thy name shall be Abraham; for a father of many nations have I made thee. And I will make thee exceeding fruitful, and I will make nations of thee, and kings shall come out of thee. *And I will establish my covenant between me and thee and thy seed after thee in their generations for an everlasting covenant, to be a God unto thee, and to thy seed after thee.* And I will give unto thee, and to thy seed after thee, the land wherein thou art a stranger, all the land of Canaan, for an everlasting possession; and I will be their God.

(Gen. 17:1-8, emphasis added)

Changing a person's name was one way that God elevated a relationship with Himself. In this instance, when God initiated a covenant with Abram, He changed his name to Abraham. He told Abraham that the covenant was also with his children. Christians are Abraham's spiritual children.

Know therefore that the LORD thy God, he [is] God, the faithful God, which keepeth covenant and mercy with them that love him and keep his commandments to a thousand generations.

(Deut. 7:9)

God told Abraham that he would have everlasting possession of the land of Canaan. As Paul states, "If ye [be] Christ's, then are ye Abraham's seed, and heirs according to the promise" (Gal. 3:29). We are inheritors of the Abrahamic covenant because we are in Jesus, who fulfills every covenant that God made.

> And God said unto Abraham, Thou shalt keep my covenant therefore, thou, and thy seed after thee in their generations. This is my covenant, which ye shall keep, between me and you and thy seed after thee; Every man child among you shall be circumcised.
>
> (Gen. 17:9-10)

God gave circumcision of the flesh as a sign that He had made covenant with Abraham and his descendants. For Christians, circumcision of the heart is God's sign of the new covenant (see Rom. 2:29). The Israelites trusted the covenant sign made in their flesh by circumcision, but they didn't maintain a proper heart attitude toward God. As a result, they lost the privilege to live in the Promised Land for many centuries.

> And he sent, and brought him in. Now he [was] ruddy, [and] withal of a beautiful countenance, and goodly to look to. And the LORD said, Arise, anoint him: for this [is] he. Then Samuel took the horn of oil, and anointed him in the midst of his brethren: and the spirit of the LORD came upon David from that day forward.
>
> (1 Sam. 16:12-13)

God established David as king over Israel by having Samuel anoint him with oil. Oil is symbolic of the Holy Spirit. God expresses His covenant with us by giving the indwelling Holy Spirit.

> Now these [be] the last words of David. David the son of Jesse said, and the man [who was] raised up on high, the anointed of the God of Jacob, and the sweet psalmist of Israel, said, The spirit of the LORD spake by me, and his word [was] in

my tongue. The God of Israel said, the Rock of Israel spake to me, He that ruleth over men [must be] just, ruling in the fear of God. And [he shall be] as the light of the morning, [when] the son riseth, [even] a morning without clouds; [as] the tender grass [springing] out of the earth by clear shining after rain. Although my house [be] not so with God; *yet he hath made with me an everlasting covenant, ordered in all [things], and sure*: for [this is] all my salvation, and all [my] desire, although he make [it] not to grow.

(2 Sam. 23:1-5, emphasis added)

God made a covenant with David in which He established all things ordered and sure. "Ordered" in this sense means to be arranged in a way that is in God's design. "Sure" means to hedge about, to guard or to protect. What God establishes, God protects. David had only to rule in submission and righteousness.

But ye have an *unction* from the Holy One, and ye know all things.

(1 John 2:20, emphasis added)

But the *anointing* which ye have received of him abideth in you, and ye need not that any man teach you: but as the same anointing teacheth you of all things, and is truth, and is no lie, and even as it hath taught you, ye shall abide in him.

(1 John 2:27, emphasis added)

The words "unction" and "anointing" are translated from the Greek *chrisma*, which refers to the anointing of the Holy Spirit. "For the gifts and calling of God are without repentance" (Rom. 11:29). "My kindness shall not depart from thee, neither shall the covenant of my peace be removed" (Isa. 54:10). God is who He is, always has been and always will be. He is the same yesterday, today and forever (see Heb. 13:8).

When God made covenant with Abram, according to the custom of that time He instructed Abram to cut three animals in half and place the halves opposite each other. A deep sleep then fell upon Abram. As Abram slept, God passed between the halves of the animals with the appearance of a smoking furnace (see Gen. 15:8). The splitting of the animals is symbolic of an irrevocable covenant.

The Word tells us that the sanctuary of God will be in our midst. The meaning of the Hebrew word translated as "midst" is "between the halves." When God says, "I AM in the midst of you," He is saying that He is fulfilling His part of the covenant. A blood covenant exists between God and Christians today. Something (Someone) had to die to ratify this covenant with blood.

> The Lord is not slack concerning his promise, as some men count slackness; but is longsuffering to us-ward, not willing that any should perish, but that all should come to repentance.
>
> (2 Pet. 3:9)

We may find it hard to keep our promises, but God has no difficulty in keeping His. If we are having problems and think that God is not keeping His promises, we can be absolutely certain that we are wrong.

> God [is] not a man, that he should lie; neither the son of man, that he should repent: hath he said and shall he not do [it]? or hath he spoken, and shall he not make it good.
>
> (Num. 23:19)

If God said He will do something, then He will do it—no ifs, ands, buts, whereases, or wherefores about it. However, God's promises are often conditional on us fulfilling our part. God expects us to honor His covenant. If we fail to meet the conditions of the covenant, we cannot expect God to fulfill the promises He made in that covenant.

> And, behold, the Lord stood above it, and said, I [am] the LORD God of Abraham thy father, and the God of Isaac: the land whereon thou liest, to thee will I give it, and to thy seed; And thy seed shall be as the dust of the earth, and thou shalt spread abroad to the west, and to the east, and to the north,

> and to the south and in thee and in thy seed shall all the families of the earth be blessed. And, behold, I [am] with thee, and will keep thee in all [places] whither thou goest, and will bring thee again into this land; for I will not leave thee, until I have done [that] which I have spoken to thee of.
>
> (Gen. 28:13-15)

In Jacob's dream, God restated the covenant promise He had first made to Abraham and extended to Jacob's father, Isaac. This dream occurred when Jacob was running for his life. Jacob, aided by the lies and manipulations of his mother, had stolen the blessing of the first-born Esau (see Genesis 27). Jacob was seriously imperfect, but God kept His promise.

God's promises are based on His grace and our heart attitude, not on our perfection. Many times, we want to do things that we can't do. Many times, we want to do things we can't do, but do them anyway (see Rom. 7:15). God does not break covenant with us because of our weakness or ignorance. God will say to some that they broke covenant with Him because of wickedness.

> And Jacob vowed a vow, saying, If God will be with me, and will keep me in this way that I go, and will give me bread to eat, and raiment to put on, So that I come again to my father's house in peace; then shall the Lord be my God; And this stone, which I have set for a pillar, shall be God's house; and of all that thou shalt give me I will surely give the tenth unto thee.
>
> (Gen. 28:20-22)

Jacob understood the dream. He agreed to the covenant that God offered to him and vowed to do what God said. God would be his God, and he would give the Lord a tenth of all that He gave Jacob. (Abraham had initiated the tithe, or the tenth part, when he gave tithes to Melchizedek in Genesis 14:18-20).

We are to render unto God that which belongs to God—submission, obedience, worship and tithes. Tithing is not an issue of Law; it is an issue of principle. By embracing this principle, I believe that we soundly defeat the spirit of Mammon, break the stronghold of materialism, and set ourselves free to be good stewards of all that God gives us. We acknowledge God as our faithful source and provider by returning to Him a tenth of what He has given to us. I believe that the tenth has always belonged to Him.

We must surrender the government of our lives to God. He shall be our God. We must submit to His will and grant Him His way.

> And Moses took half of the blood, and put [it] in basins; and half of the blood he sprinkled on the altar. And he took the book of the covenant, and read in the audience of the people: and they said, All that the LORD hath said will we do, and be obedient. And Moses took the blood, and sprinkled [it] on the people, and said, Behold the blood of the covenant, which the LORD hath made with you concerning all these words.
>
> (Ex. 24:6-8)

If we are in Jesus, we are under the blood. Jesus' death ratified a blood covenant between God and His people.

> And if it seem evil unto you to serve the LORD, choose you this day whom ye will serve; whether the gods which your fathers served that were on the other side of the flood, or the gods of the Amorites, in whose land ye dwell: but as for me and my house, we will serve the LORD.
>
> (Josh. 24:15)

> And the people said unto Joshua, The LORD our God will we serve, and his voice will we obey. So Joshua made a covenant with the people that day, and set them a statute and an ordinance in Shechem.
>
> (Josh. 24:24-25)

Covenant requires that we decide whom we shall serve. The Israelites acknowledged the covenant and reaffirmed who they were and what that meant. If we desire to be in covenant with God, we must do the same.

> And the king stood by a pillar, and made a covenant before the LORD, to walk after the LORD, and to keep his commandments and his testimonies and his statutes with all [their] heart and all [their] soul, to perform the words of this covenant that were written in this book. And all the people stood to the covenant.
>
> (2 Kings 23:3)

When the covenant was proclaimed, King Josiah inquired of the people what they were going to do about it. In response, they stood up as a sign of having entered into the covenant. "Stood" in this context means to acknowledge, to join in, or to agree to something. Have we likewise "stood" to the covenant ratified in the blood of Jesus, or are we equivocating?

> And they entered into a covenant to seek the LORD God of their fathers *with all their heart and with all their soul.*
> (2 Chron. 15:12, emphasis added)

A covenant can never be halfway. We either have a whole covenant, or we have no covenant. This is the implication of Revelation 3:16: "So then because thou art lukewarm, and neither cold nor hot, I will spew thee out of my mouth." We can't have half a covenant with Jesus. He didn't give half of His life, and we can't give Him half of ours.

> And the rest of the people, the priests, the Levites, the porters, the singers, the Nethinims, and all they that had separated themselves from the people of the lands unto the law of God, their wives, their sons, and their daughters, every one having knowledge, and having understanding; They clave to their brethren, their nobles, and entered into a curse, and into an oath, to walk in God's law, which was given by Moses the servant of God, and to observe and do all the commandments of the LORD our Lord, and his judgments and his statutes.
> (Neh. 10:28-29)

The book of Ezra tells about the restoration of the Temple. The book of Nehemiah records the rebuilding of the walls and the gates of Jerusalem. These two events symbolize God's rebuilding and restoration of His Church. God does not intend to renew *our* church; He is committed to rebuilding and restoring *His* Church. He will not be deterred in this effort, for if He encounters obstacles, He will simply circumvent or remove them. An essential component of this rebuilding and restoration is for us to honor the covenant we have with the Lord and with one another.

We are not half-saved. We do not half belong to God. We don't have half a covenant. Likewise, it is not appropriate for us to be half-obedient. The covenant we have with God is mutually exclusive and does not allow for halfway measures. God intends that His covenant be embraced completely.

> When thou shalt vow a vow unto the LORD thy God, thou shalt not slack to pay it: for the LORD thy God will surely require it of thee; and it would be sin in thee.
>
> (Deut. 23:21)

We can't make promises to God and then not fulfill those promises. We must keep our vow (covenant) with God. If we don't, we sin. Every one of us has made promises to God and then neglected them, but God does not forget. A day of reckoning will come when the Lord will ask if we will or will not keep our promises. A day is coming when the road we are traveling will come to a T-intersection. We will have to turn left or right. Otherwise, we will be unable to continue.

I believe that the day is not far off when we will reach that T-intersection. The restoration coming to God's Church will not allow for double-mindedness. We will either fully participate or we will be left out. I don't mean that we will lose our salvation—I mean that we will miss out on what God is doing in the restoration of His Church and the advancing of His kingdom.

In his book *Houses That Change The World*, Wolfgang Simson points out that there are four paths for church growth: (1) we build our church; (2) we ask Jesus to build our church; (3) we try to build His Church; or (4) Jesus builds His Church. Simson says that all four paths are successful to some degree, but only the fourth path has the fullness of the life that God intends.

> Take my yoke upon you, and learn of me; for I am meek and lowly in heart: and ye shall find rest unto your souls. For my yoke [is] easy, and my burden is light.
>
> (Matt. 11:29-30)

We are yoked to Jesus. A yoke rests on the shoulders. It is a constraint in the sense that it joins us to one another and limits us in what we can do individually. One can imagine what would happen if the person with whom we are yoked begins skipping and jumping. We would be pulled off course and lose our balance, and our forward progress would be hindered.

When we tell Jesus that He is Lord, we pledge to accept the responsibility that comes with being yoked to Him. We affirm our covenant with Him, which means we must walk in unity with Him. If we don't accept (yield to) His yoke, we break covenant with Him.

If we each have covenant with Jesus, it is not difficult to understand that covenant also exists between believers. God invented mathematics. One of the axioms of plane geometry is "things equal to the same thing are equal to each other." If A equals B and B equals C, it follows that C and A are equal. Covenant follows the same logic. The cross is a symbol of covenant; it has a vertical and a horizontal beam. The vertical speaks of our covenant with the Lord, while the horizontal speaks of our covenant with other believers. If either part is missing, we no longer have the cross.

God teaches that everything we say and do affects everyone around us. A chain consists of many individual links that are joined together. We cannot pick up one link without affecting the entire chain. Likewise, Christians cannot have an individualistic mentality. The conduct of one believer affects the whole Body of Christ. Covenant makes each Christian an integral part of a much greater whole. When a covenant relationship is broken, something is torn from our lives. We feel the loss—and so does the Lord Jesus.

If we try to hammer a nail but hit our thumb instead, every part of our body will feel the pain. Our mouth will have something to say; our eyes will water and our feet will move. We will jump around, hoot, wave and do all sorts of things in response to that pain. So it is in the Body of Christ. If one is injured, all should feel the injury.

> Now I beseech you, brethren, by the name of our Lord Jesus Christ, that ye all speak the same thing, and [that] there be no divisions among you; but [that] ye be perfectly joined together in the same mind and in the same judgment.
>
> (1 Cor. 1:10)

"Perfectly joined together" means strongly completed. "Mind" means thought, feeling, will, and understanding. "Judgment" means opinion or resolve. All of these point to willingness and determination to be unified by the Spirit.

> But he that is joined unto the Lord is one Spirit.
>
> (1 Cor. 6:17)

The word "joined" means superglued. Covenant makes us inseparable. The animals that were cut in half when God made covenant with Abram could not be put back together. The shed blood could not be returned to restore them to life in order to void the covenant. Covenant is a one-way street. Once we enter in, we are in permanently. Through our sin we may break a covenant, but we remain accountable to that covenant.

> From whom the whole body fitly joined together and compacted by that which every joint supplieth, according to the effectual working in the measure of every part, maketh increase of the body unto the edifying of itself in love.
>
> (Eph. 4:16)

"Fitly joined together" can be understood as stones fitted together and held in place by mortar. Individual believers are building stones that God uses to build His Church. Our spiritual shape and size defines where we are placed and how we fit in relation to those around us. If we don't fit with the other stones around us, the structure is out of kilter. This is why the Word says, "But now hath God set the members every one of them in the body as it hath pleased him" (1 Cor. 12:18). We don't have the choice of where we are placed in the Body of Christ—God sets us in our place. It is our covenant responsibility to recognize that place, go there, and show ourselves faithful.

Our covenant with God requires that we remain where He places us and not go wandering on our own whim from one fellowship to another. God desires that we settle where He places us and interact with the people around us to be fitly joined together. God is building *His* Church. If the stone that we represent is out of place or missing, we are not fulfilling our horizontal covenant or functioning as God intends.

> [Be] of the same mind one toward another. Mind not high things, but condescend to men of low estate. Be not wise in your own conceits.
>
> (Rom. 12:16)

We must think as highly of others as we do of ourselves. We must think rationally, reasonably, and accurately about ourselves and not be puffed up (see Rom. 12:3). Our covenant with God is one of acknowledging His Lordship and being obedient to Him. If we violate any part of this, we violate the covenant.

> Finally, brethren, farewell. *Be* perfect, *be* of good comfort, *be* of one mind, live in peace; and the God of love and peace shall be with you.
>
> (2 Cor. 13:11, emphasis added)

The word "be" is an imperative, a command, and not a suggestion. Paul doesn't say that it would be good if the believers at Corinth lived in peace—he directs them to do it. The difference between something being good if we do it and actually doing it requires a decision and a commitment to be faithful to covenant.

> Finally, [be ye] all of one mind, having compassion one of another, love as brethren, [be] pitiful, [be] courteous.
>
> (1 Pet. 3:8)

Many Christians don't understand true unity. When they talk about unity, they do not talk about covenant but rather compromise, the lowest common denominator. They ignore the truth of God to achieve a false peace. When we agree with what God says and stand committed to Jesus in covenant, we will experience true oneness with Him and with one another.

In the Old Testament, when the Israelites built a Temple according to the pattern that had been given to them by God, the Lord filled it with the glory (*Shekinah*) of His presence (see Ex. 40:33-35 and 1 Kings 8:10-11). Today, God is building a House where He will live, not just visit (see Eph. 2:19). "The glory of this latter house shall be greater than of the former" (Hag. 2:9). The Church will be rebuilt and restored. God's glory will fill it if it is built according to His pattern—a pattern that begins with our keeping covenant with God and with each other.

> Can two walk together, except they be agreed?
>
> (Amos 3:3)

The word "agreed" means by mutual consent. It literally means to be engaged to be married. Jesus will return for His Bride, but if the Bridegroom is saying one thing and the Bride is saying something else, they are not walking in agreement. It is like running in a three-legged race with someone who is attempting to go in a different direction.

> I will go into thy house with burnt offerings: I will pay thee my vows, Which my lips have uttered, and my mouth hath spoken, when I was in trouble.
>
> (Ps. 66:13-14)

We often make promises when we find ourselves in a bad situation and want God to get us out of trouble. However, we need to remember that God will accept our vow as a covenant. The vow exists within the context of covenant. God does not forget the promises we make, even if we forget.

I recall the testimony of a man who had been on a troop ship during World War II. His ship was torpedoed and sank in the North Atlantic, where the water temperatures in the winter could cause death by hypothermia in minutes. When he hit the water, he cried out to the Lord and said, "God, if You save me, I'll serve you the rest of my life." When the next wave swept over him and he surfaced again, he found that there was a life raft right next to him that hadn't been there before. I was in a meeting with this man when, 45 years later, God reminded him of his promise. The man was devastated—but forgiven.

> The earth also is defiled under the inhabitants thereof; because they have transgressed the laws, changed the ordinance, broken the everlasting covenant.
>
> (Isa. 24:5)

Even the earth is defiled when people oppose God's will and change the divine order by deciding to do what they please or changing the meaning of what God has said. In so doing, they break covenant.

> And the uncircumcised man-child whose flesh of his foreskin is not circumcised, that soul shall be cut off from his people; he hath broken my covenant.
>
> (Gen. 17:14)

> And it came to pass by the way in the inn, that the LORD met him, and sought to kill him. Then Zipporah took a sharp stone, and cut off the foreskin of her son, and cast [it] at his feet, and said, Surely a bloody husband [art] thou to me. So he let him go; then she said, A bloody husband [thou art], because of the circumcision.
>
> (Ex. 4:24-26)

When God told Moses to go to Pharaoh, Moses set out to obey, but then apparently his wife, Zipporah, talked him out of circumcising their son. The anger of the Lord burned against Moses because he did not fulfill the covenant requirement. The

Lord sought to kill him and brought him so close to death that Zipporah realized that she had better change her mind.

Consider the powers of evil that Moses would have to face in Egypt when he went up against Pharaoh's magicians and soothsayers. God released His power and authority through Moses' spoken word and his extended rod. We can understand how much importance God placed on His covenant with Moses. If Moses had been disobedient, the demonic powers would have used that opportunity to oppose and prevent the will of God being done through him.

> For he is not a Jew, which is one outwardly; neither [is that] circumcision, which is outward in the flesh: But he [is] a Jew, which is one inwardly; and circumcision [is that] of the heart, in the spirit, [and] not in the letter; whose praise [is] not of men, but of God.
>
> (Rom. 2:28-29)

Covenant includes obedience to God's will and conformity to His ways. Paul compares the Spirit and the flesh, saying that a Jew can be circumcised in the flesh but not be a true Jew if his heart is not right. A Gentile who is circumcised in his heart can be a truer Jew than a Jew who is circumcised in the flesh because the Gentile's heart is right and his relationship is right before God.

Appearance, religious behavior or the observance of rules does not make one a Christian. It is heart attitude in covenant relationship. To be circumcised in the heart means we keep our covenant with God—not in the letter of the law but in the Spirit. God expects us to put His kingdom and His righteousness first (see Matt. 6:33). The Lord's Prayer is structured that way. First, we ask for God's kingdom to come and His will to be done. Second, we ask Him to meet our needs, give us our daily bread, forgive us our sins and protect us (see Luke 11:2-4). We are not to please men but to be people who please God (see Eph. 6:6-7).

> For thus saith the LORD GOD; I will even deal with thee as thou hast done, which hast despised the oath in breaking the covenant. Nevertheless I will remember my covenant with thee in the days of thy youth, and I will establish unto thee an everlasting covenant.
>
> (Ezek. 16:59-60)

God deals firmly and decisively with covenant breakers. God will continue to affirm that He will remember His covenant. He will continue honoring it even when we break it. His covenant is everlasting.

> If my people, which are called by my name, shall humble themselves, and pray, and seek my face, and turn from their wicked ways; then will I hear from heaven, and will forgive their sin, and will heal their land.
>
> (2 Chron. 7:14)

If we don't meet the covenant conditions, God is not obligated to keep the covenant promises. We are supposed to humble ourselves, seek His face, turn from our wicked ways, and pray. His part is conditional on us our doing our part.

Jesus said that His judgment (discernment) was accurate because He did not seek to do His own will but rather the will of God who sent Him (see John 5:30). If we are not keeping covenant with one another and not in the place where God wants us, we are not fulfilling covenant with God. To keep covenant, we must mortify the deeds of the flesh (see Rom. 8:13) and deny self's attempts to govern our lives (see Matt. 16:24).

Chapter 9

DEATH

Have you ever considered that death is both an event and a process? Do you comprehend that the keys for both the event and the process of death are in the hands of the Lord?

People are instinctively afraid of physical death and compulsively seek what the world calls self-fulfillment. However, physical death and death to self-life are both advancement in the kingdom of God. Physical death moves Christians to heaven to be with Jesus. We progress spiritually as we die to self-centeredness and self-government.

> Behold, the days come, saith the LORD, that I will make a new covenant with the house of Israel, and with the house of Judah; Not according to the covenant that I made with their fathers in the day [that] I took them by the hand to bring them out of the land of Egypt; which my covenant they brake, although I was an husband unto them, saith the LORD: But this [shall be] the covenant that I will make with the house of Israel; After those days, saith the LORD, *I will put my law in their inward parts, and write it in their hearts*; and will be their God, and they shall be my people.
>
> (Jer. 31:31-33, emphasis added)

The Hebrews considered the heart to be the innermost part of a human being. The Greek word for "heart" is *nous*, which included a person's thought processes, feelings, attitudes, and motives. These can be considered to be functions of a person's innermost being or heart.

God's new covenant is better than the old covenant that was based on the Law. The Law was never able to bring anyone to righteousness; it only identified sin. Paul said, "For I was alive without the law once: but when the commandment came, sin revived, and I died" (Rom. 7:9). Paul realized that he could not keep the Law perfectly even though he was a Pharisee and the son of a Pharisee (see Acts 23:6). Being compelled to be perfect by the Law is an unbearable burden.

> The Lord is not slack concerning his promise, as some men count slackness; but is longsuffering to us-ward, not willing that any should perish, but that all should come to repentance.
>
> (2 Pet. 3:9)

> God [is] not a man, that he should lie; neither the son of man, that he should repent; hath he said, and shall he not do [it]? or hath he spoken, and shall he not make it good?
>
> (Num. 23:19)

God is not negligent regarding the promises He made in the new covenant. We can be certain He will do what He says He will do.

> For this is my blood of the New Testament, which is shed for many for the remission of sins.
>
> (Matt. 26:28)

"Testament" is another word for covenant. The new covenant was sealed and ratified by the blood of Jesus.

> But now hath he obtained a more excellent ministry, by how much also he is the mediator of a better covenant, which was established upon better promises.
>
> (Heb. 8:6)

> And to Jesus the mediator of the new covenant, and to the
> blood of the sprinkling, [that] speaketh better things than
> that of Abel.
>
> (Heb. 12:24)

Jesus is the mediator because His blood was the seal of the covenant. He was the sacrifice that validated the covenant. A mediator is a go-between. Only One who is wholly God and wholly human can bridge the chasm between God and sinful people. God knew before time began that a bridge would be needed. He ordained that Jesus would be that bridge. This is why Jesus is called the Lamb of God slain from the foundation of the world (see Rev. 13:8).

> Now the God of peace, that brought again from the dead our
> Lord Jesus, that great shepherd of the sheep, through the
> blood of the everlasting covenant.
>
> (Heb. 13:20)

The blood of Christ sealed the everlasting covenant; the last one God will make with His people. God made one change from the old covenant to the new covenant, which is in Jesus.

> But Christ being come an high priest of good things to come,
> by a greater and more perfect tabernacle, not made with
> hands, that is to say, not of this building; Neither by the blood
> of goats and calves, but by his own blood he entered in once
> into the holy place, having obtained eternal redemption [for
> us].
>
> (Heb. 9:11-12)

In Old Testament times, the high priest entered the Holy of Holies once a year and sprinkled the blood of an animal on the mercy seat on top of the Ark of the Covenant. This blood atoned for the sins the people of Israel had committed during the past year. The high priest prefigured Jesus, who entered the Holy of Holies in heaven—a place prepared by God by His Word. Jesus sprinkled His blood there to atone for all sins for all eternity.

> How much more shall the blood of Christ, who through the
> eternal Spirit offered himself without spot to God, purge your
> conscience from dead works to serve the living God? And for
> this cause he is the mediator of the New Testament, that by
> means of death, for the redemption of the transgressions [that
> were] under the first testament, they which are called might
> receive the promise of eternal inheritance.
>
> (Heb. 9:14-15)

One party offers to make covenant—that is God. The other
party responds—that is God's people. Jesus fulfilled His part of
the covenant by laying down His life. In response, we must lay
down our lives (self-life) and fulfill our part of the covenant. The
Greek language has three words for life: *bios*, which is physical
life; *psuche,* which is essentially soul life; and *zoe,* which is spirit
life.

> But Jesus called them [unto him], and said, Ye know that the
> princes of the Gentiles exercise dominion over them, and
> they that are great exercise authority upon them. But it shall
> not be so among you: but whosoever will be great among you,
> let him be your minister; And whosoever will be chief among
> you, let him be your servant: Even as the Son of man came
> not to be ministered unto, but to minister, and to give his life
> a ransom for many.
>
> (Matt. 20:25-28)

In this passage, Jesus was speaking about His death but was
emphasizing His place as a servant. He wasn't speaking only
about His physical life but also the laying down of *psuche*—His
will, His desires, and His personal feelings—so that He might be
a servant. He set the example for us.

> Greater love hath no man than this, that a man lay down his
> life for his friends.
>
> (John 15:13)

The word translated as "life" in this verse is *psuche,* or soul
life. If we lay down our desires, ambitions and agendas and

consecrate our lives to the service of God and others, this is the greatest act of love. *Psuche* can include physical life in some contexts.

> The thief cometh not, but for to steal, and to kill, and to destroy; I am come that they might have life and that they might have it more abundantly.
>
> (John 10:10)

Here the word translated as "life" is *zoe*. Jesus came to give us spiritual life. His death and resurrection released that spiritual life to us.

> I am the good shepherd, and know my [sheep], and am known of mine. As the Father knoweth me, even so know I the Father: and I lay down my life for the sheep. And other sheep I have, which are not of this fold: them also I must bring, and they shall hear my voice; and there shall be one fold, [and] one shepherd. Therefore doth my Father love me, because I lay down my life, that I might take it again.
>
> (John 10:14-17)

In these verses, Jesus is again talking about laying down soul-life or self-centered life. He came to earth to do the will of the Father, spoke what the Father told Him to speak, and worked at whatever task the Father gave Him. He lived in submission to the Father. He also laid down His *bios*, or physical life—the final blood sacrifice required to fulfill the Law.

> Hereby perceive we the love [of God], because he laid down his life for us: and we ought to lay down our lives for the brethren.
>
> (1 John 3:16)

Jesus laid down His soul-life (ambition, personal identity, and agenda) for us. In response, we ought to lay down our soul life (personal identity, desires, agenda, and ambition) for Him and for each other.

> For the Son of man is not come to destroy men's lives, but to
> save [them].
>
> (Luke 9:56)

The Son of Man did not come to destroy our *psuche* lives or
to force us to become slaves. He came to save us from our sin.
We occasionally think that God asks too much of us. But do we
ever ask too much of God?

> And he said to [them] all, If any [man] will come after me, let
> him deny himself, and take his cross daily, and follow me. For
> whosoever will save his life shall lose it: but whosoever will
> lose his life for my sake, the same shall save it.
>
> (Luke 9:23-24)

To "deny" in this sense means to disown, to forget or to lose
sight of something. Jesus is referring to self, which is our soul-life
or self-centered and self-governing identity. We are to choose
to deny, disown, forget, and lose sight of ourselves and our self-
centeredness and take up our cross daily. The cross is not just
a symbol of Christianity; it is an instrument of death. Whoever
loses his life (self-life) for Jesus' sake shall find (spiritual) life
(see Matthew 10:39).

> Then Jesus beholding him loved him, and said unto him, *One*
> *thing thou lackest:* go thy way, sell whatsoever thou hast, and
> give to the poor, and thou shalt have treasure in heaven: and
> come, take up the cross, and follow me. And he was sad at that
> saying, and went away grieved: for he had great possessions.
>
> (Mark 10:21-22, emphasis added)

In this story told in Mark, the wealthy young man had ob-
served the commandments, kept the Law and done everything
he thought was required to lead a righteous life. However, he
was unwilling to relinquish his possessions. As a result, he did
not receive all of God's benefits. Jesus said the young man wasn't
willing to walk away from his wealth, from which he derived his

self-life, his identity and his security. The problem was not his wealth; it was that he put his trust in his wealth.

> Therefore I say unto you, Take no thought for your life, what ye shall eat, or what ye shall drink; nor yet for your body, what ye shall put on. Is not the life more than meat, and the body than raiment?
>
> (Matt. 6:25)

Jesus says that we should take no thought for our *psuche*, our self-life, self-centeredness and selfish ambition. This includes not worrying about basic needs. If we make daily needs our priority, we will miss out what actually matters—the fullness of God's kingdom. Making our needs a priority over our obligations to God is a form of idolatry!

Someone once told me that the area of the brain that generates worry is also the same part of the brain that generates prayer. So if we are worrying, we are not praying, and if we are not praying, we are relying on our strength instead of on God's strength. That is why Paul exhorted us to be anxious for nothing but pray about everything (see Philippians 4:6).

> According to my earnest expectation and [my] hope, that in nothing I shall be ashamed, but [that] with all boldness, as always, so now also Christ shall be magnified in my body, whether [it be] by life, or by death. For to me to live [is] Christ, and to die [is] gain. For I am in a strait betwixt two, having a desire to depart, and to be with Christ; which is far better: Nevertheless to abide in the flesh [is] more needful for you.
>
> (Phil. 1:21-24)

Paul said he would prefer to leave the world in physical death to go and be with Jesus, but he knew he had not yet finished what God had intended for him to do. Therefore, he was willing to remain on earth, despite all his suffering and hardships, to serve others. Escape is seldom the will of God; standing firm is His will (see Eph. 6.10-14).

That I may know him, and the power of his resurrection, and the fellowship of his sufferings, being made conformable unto his death.

(Phil. 3:10)

Paul wanted to live a worthy life and be so like Jesus that he could sacrifice his life as Jesus did. (He eventually died a martyr for the kingdom of God.) He also wanted to be conformed to the character of Jesus so that his whole life (*psuche*) would be yielded to the Father. He had one purpose in life: to fulfill the will of God. Therefore, conformance to Jesus' death means that we will be conformed to His life. We cannot fully entire the new life of God and follow Him unless we are willing to depart from the old life (see Ephesians 4:22-24).

I can of my own self do nothing: as I hear, I judge: and my judgment is just; because I seek not mine own will, but the will of the Father which hath sent me.

(John 5:30)

In this verse, "judge" and "judgment" mean discerning truth, not rendering verdicts. Jesus subordinated His will to that of the Father. He could see clearly the Father's plan and purpose.

I once asked the Lord how He defined confusion. I believe His answer was, "Confusion is the evidence of the presence of more than one will." For Jesus, there was never any confusion. He was never double-minded. When Satan tempted Him to use heavenly power for His own personal benefit, Jesus responded that He would do nothing apart from the Father. He denied ambition and refused to allow His will to operate apart from the will of the Father. Jesus' will was fully submitted to the will of the Father (see John 6:38).

Then said Jesus unto them, When ye have lifted up the Son of man, then shall ye know that I am he, and that I do nothing of myself; but as my Father hath taught me, I speak these things. And he that sent me is with me; the Father hath not left me alone; for I do always those things that please him.

(John 8:28-29)

Jesus denied Himself to please the Father and to serve us. What a life we would have if we would do the same! People today often tell others to "get a life." Becoming like Jesus is the only way to experience true life.

> For I have not spoken of myself; but the Father which sent me, he gave me a commandment, what I should say, and what I should speak. And I know that his commandment is life everlasting: whatsoever I speak therefore, even as the Father said unto, so I speak.
>
> (John 12:49-50)

Jesus denied His self-importance. What would our lives be like if we spoke only what the Lord gave us to speak? We would probably speak less impulsively, create less strife, and give less offense to others.

> Who, being in the form of God, thought it not robbery to be equal with God: But made himself of no reputation, and took upon him the form of a servant, and was made in the likeness of men.
>
> (Phil. 2:6-7)

Jesus denied self-exaltation. He willingly took the low place and did not seek reputation.

> And now, O Father, glorify thou me with thine own self with the glory which I had with thee before the world was.
>
> (John 17:5)

Jesus denied personal ambition. Just imagine for a moment what Jesus had to leave to come to earth and become a human being. It was an incredible step down from the Throne of Glory. Not only that, He made Himself the lowest of men—a foot-washing servant.

> Not that I speak in respect of want: for I have learned, in whatsoever state I am, [therewith] to be content. I know both

how to be abased, and I know how to be abound; every where
and in all things I am instructed both to be full and to be hun-
gry, both to abound and to suffer need.

(Phil. 4:11-12)

Jesus denied personal gratification. Paul said that because of
Jesus, he could go anywhere, do anything, and be anything. He
could have excess or lack, and it made no difference to him. He
had learned to be content. This attitude cannot be taught; it is
formed through experience.

I am crucified with Christ: nevertheless I live; yet not I, but
Christ liveth in me: and the life which I now live in the flesh
I live by the faith of the Son of God, who loved me, and gave
himself for me.

(Gal. 2:20)

Paul understood that a substitution had been made. He knew
that he had been bought with a price and that because of this
he was no longer his own (see 1 Corinthians 6:19-20). Paul also
grasped another concept: he had forsaken his self-life to gain
the life of Christ.

Knowing this, that our old man is crucified with [him], that
the body of sin might be destroyed, that henceforth we should
not serve sin. For he that is dead is freed from sin. Now if we
be dead with Christ, we believe that we shall also live with
him.

(Rom. 6:6-8)

Our old self, the Adam nature, was crucified and died with
Jesus. We are now risen with Him and live with Him in new life.
These are accomplished facts that we haven't yet fully experienced. The word "believe" in this passage means that we are so
fully persuaded of this truth that our focus and energy is devoted
to living the new life.

And you, that were sometime alienated and enemies in [your] mind by wicked works, yet now hath he reconciled in the body of his flesh through death, to present you holy and unblameable and unreproveable in his sight: If ye continue in the faith grounded and settled, and [be] not moved away from the hope of the gospel, which ye have heard, [and] which was preached to every creature which is under heaven; whereof I Paul am made a minister.

(Col. 1:21-23)

Paul laid his life down for the Church. The Church is not an organizational structure. It is the organism called the Body of Christ that is comprised of true believers worldwide. We don't serve a building, an organization, or a hierarchy. We serve God and one another. "For, brethren, ye have been called unto liberty; only use not liberty for an occasion to the flesh, but by love serve one another" (Gal. 5:13).

Always bearing about in the body the dying of the Lord Jesus, that the life also of Jesus might be made manifest in our body. For we which live are always delivered unto death for Jesus' sake, that the life also of Jesus might be made manifest in our mortal flesh. So then death worketh in us, but life in you.

(2 Cor. 4:10-12)

Paul's statement appears to be illogical. How can death be working in us if we are alive? It obviously cannot mean physical death. It means death to our self-governed life. We die daily to our self-life so that Jesus' life may be manifested through us. We give up our self-centered and individualistic life so that we can display the character of Jesus. This allows the life of Jesus in us to work effectively on behalf of others. It is not our death to self-life that ministers to people but the life of Jesus that replaces it. We cannot minister effectively with only the power of our self-life.

But what think ye? A [certain] man had two sons; and he came to the first, and said, Son, go work today in my vineyard. He answered and said, I will not: but afterward he repented,

and went. And he came to the second, and said likewise. And
he answered and said, I [go], sir: and went not. Whether of
them twain did the will of [his] father? They say unto him,
The first. Jesus saith unto them, Verily I say unto you, That
the publicans and the harlots go into the kingdom of God
before you.

(Matt. 21:28-31)

In this parable that Jesus told to His followers, the first son, in
his self-life, said he didn't want to work in the vineyard. However,
after thinking about it, he changed his mind and concluded that
his father had the right to ask him to work. He agreed to submit
his life and ambition to his father and reject the desire to spend
the day in leisure. Jesus said this son fulfilled the will of the father. Although the first son had initially objected, he eventually
decided to work in the vineyard. The second son, however, did
just the opposite: When asked to work said he would but then
changed his mind. He didn't go to the vineyard in spite of the
fact that he told his father he would.

Jesus told the religious leaders of the day that publicans and
harlots, the people most despised, would enter the kingdom of
God before them. The publicans and harlots knew they needed
to repent and were not self-righteousness. They realized that they
had to give up everything to fulfill the will of the Father. Is our
present way of life worth keeping? Or do we need to exchange
it for God's better way? We must continually choose which life
we prefer: Jesus' or our own. That choice will then determine
how we live. Every choice is a test.

For the love of Christ constraineth us; because we thus judge,
that if one died for all, then were all dead: And [that] he died
for all, that *they which live should not henceforth live unto themselves* but unto him which died for them, and rose again.

(2 Cor. 5:14-15, emphasis added)

Jesus is our reason for living. Jesus is our power and strength,
and Christlikeness is our objective. We should totally reject
self-centered living. The Word of God says we are dead in Jesus,

having died to our old sin-nature through Jesus' death. Through the resurrection of Jesus, we are alive as a new creation. The Word says we have a new sinless life, but experience tells us that we are not sinless. This is not a contradiction. The Word of God is without error and complete in all that it says. The apparent contradiction exists because we haven't received through experience what the Bible says—that we are dead to sin and alive in Jesus.

We will not have complete spiritual victory unless we terminate our self-centeredness. Satan cannot tempt or trouble a dead person. Jesus could face the prince of this world and say Satan had nothing in Him because He was completely dead to self-life. Satan could not reach Him by tempting Him with desires arising from the flesh or the soul. Jesus lived fully in the Spirit, so Satan couldn't touch Him.

We must take strong action by the Spirit against everything within us that is in opposition to the rule of God. We must command our soul (mind, will, and emotions) to *get off the throne*. We must require our mind, will, and emotions to serve, not govern, and refuse them any life-governing function.

John the Baptist said, "I must decrease that He might increase" (John 3:30). The more we deny our self-will—*I want, I think, I feel, I like, I'm centered on me* —the more we will be alive in Jesus and the more His life will rule and reign in us. When we die physically, the world says that is the end. However, Paul says that for him to live is Jesus and for him to die is gain (see Phil. 1:21). We gain in death because Satan can do nothing with a corpse. If we deny our self-life we can say, "Satan, you have nothing in me." When we deny our self, nothing will remain for the evil one to pervert.

If we want victory—we must die! If we want to overcome the power of sin—we must die! If we want resurrection life—we must die! If we want life in Jesus—we must die! We will then increase in Christlikeness. That will bring victory.

Chapter 10

VICTORY

Do you always feel victorious? Or do you sometimes feel defeated? Are you overcoming, or are you being overwhelmed?

Victory means that a battle has been fought and won. Jesus achieved total victory for us through His death and resurrection. Victory for a believer is success in the war against the world, the flesh, and the Devil. We must be diligent, aware of the enemy's tactics, and persevere to live as victorious Christians. Our first challenge as Christians is to overcome the influence of the world system that Satan has constructed as a scheme to tempt us to live by the direction and power of our soul.

> For whatsoever is born of God overcometh the world: and this is the victory that overcometh the world, even our faith. Who is he that overcometh the world, but he that believeth that Jesus is the Son of God?
>
> (1 John 5:4-5)

When we were born-again, God gave us His power to overcome. Every victory we win releases us to become more alive to Jesus. We are victorious because He is our victory. We will not have victory in any part of us that is not given over to the lordship of Jesus. Praise be to God that we can grow in His victory!

> Ye adulterers and adulteresses, know ye not that the friendship of the world is enmity with God? whosoever therefore will be a friend of the world is the enemy of God.
>
> (James 4:4)

"Friend" means to have companionship and fellowship. Believers can't have friendship (agreement) with the world systems and values and be God's children. We are not supposed to participate in or agree with ungodly activities.

> Love not the world, neither the things that are in the world. If any man love the world, the love of the Father is not in him. For all that is in the world, the lust of the flesh, and the lust of the eyes, and the pride of life, is not of the Father, but is of the world. And the world passeth away, and the lust thereof: but he that doeth the will of God abideth for ever.
>
> (1 John 2:15-17)

If we love something, we earnestly desire it. Our new spiritual nature loves God and rejects the world systems. Our old self-nature loves the world and wants to cling to its fleshly pleasures and desires.

Paul recognized that he had two natures. One loved and was totally committed to God, while the other wanted to continue having its way. In this duality, he saw who he was and who he wanted to be. His earnest desire, imperfect in experience, was to serve the Lord with a whole heart (see Rom. 7:23-24).

Paul lamented that his sin-self caused him to do what he didn't want to do and prevented him from doing what he wanted to do. He wrote, "There is therefore now no condemnation to them which are in Christ Jesus" (Rom. 8:1). He understood that he had not completely overcome his sin-self, but he also knew that God didn't condemn him because of that. He knew what he wanted to do for God, but contrary behavior came from that part of him in which sin still had influence. The Devil could still trouble him through the part his self-nature that had not yet gone to the cross.

> These things I have spoken unto you, that in me ye might have peace. In the world ye shall have tribulation: but be of good cheer; I have overcome the world.
>
> (John 16:33)

We experience this truth as Jesus' life increases and our self-lives diminish. We overcome the world to the degree that we have the likeness and character of Jesus. God would never tell us to overcome the world if it were impossible, nor would He ever call us to be victorious in all that we say and do if it were not possible. So we first must have victory over the world.

The second arena of conflict is our flesh, our lower (self-centered), carnal nature. We must reject (deny) our self-governing and self-centered way of life and daily pick up our cross. Self is to no longer rule our lives. The Spirit of God should govern and direct us (see Rom. 8:14).

> And he said to them all, If any man will come after me, let him deny himself, and take up his cross daily, and follow me.
>
> (Luke 9:23)

In this verse, Jesus is saying we must allow the cross to consistently operate on our flesh (carnal nature). If we persist, we will ultimately be conformed to His likeness. As with Jesus, our flesh will not go to the cross until it has passed through Gethsemane, where our will is laid down.

We can look forward to the time when the world and everything in it will end and only the kingdom of God will remain. However, we can be free of the world and its temptations today. We can enjoy much of God's kingdom in our present life as we conform ourselves to Jesus.

Many Christians interpret much of the Bible from a futuristic perspective. This approach implies that we can't have the victory or the perfection of Christlikeness today and that we must wait until death for fulfillment of the promises of God's kingdom. This leaves us with no present hope. It results in many Christians figuratively sitting in a waiting room, holding their tickets (salvation) while waiting to enter heaven. That is not victory. It is minimal survival.

> If ye then be *risen with Christ* seek those things which are above, where Christ sitteth on the right hand of God. Set your affection on things above not on things on the earth. For ye are dead, *and your life is hid with Christ in God.* When Christ, [who is] our life, shall appear, then shall ye also appear with him in glory. Mortify therefore your members which are upon the earth; fornication, uncleanness, inordinate affection, evil concupiscence, (evil desires) and covetousness, which is idolatry.
>
> (Col. 3:1-5, emphasis added)

The word "hid" means concealed with a covering. If we are risen with Jesus, we have risen from death (dead in our sins). Our lives are hidden with Jesus in God the Father. The phrase "set your affection" means to consider, establish and direct ourselves toward an objective. In other words, we must focus and aim for heavenly objectives. Often, we do not progress as we should because we are not aiming at the higher target. In Galatians 3:27, Paul tells us to "put on Christ." "Put on" means to sink down into luxuriousness. It is like putting on a soft, warm garment—total luxury.

In Colossians 3:5, Paul says we are to *mortify* our worldly behavior. This doesn't mean to suppress our worldly desires, but rather to put them to death. We may have ideas that are good from a worldly perspective, but when compared to God's ideas, they are not good. We want and hope for many things that may appear good, but if they are contrary to the will of God, they are not good. If we have good ideas that substitute for God's will, they are evil. If we oppose God's will, that is evil. If we substitute our will for God's will, that is evil. Our religiously informed soul, apart from the Spirit, can do great harm.

1 John 2:18 says, "Even now are there many antichrists." The lowercase "christ" comes from the Greek word *christos,* which means "anointing or anointed." "Anti" can mean substitute, counterfeit, or opposing. If our soul seeks to substitute, counterfeit,

or oppose the anointing (will) of God, it means that an antichrist spirit is influencing us.

Therefore, the only good is what conforms to God's will. The Word tells us that the secret to victory is to take away life and expression from everything that is not in conformance with the will of God. We can tell the Lord that we want to give Him our lives but then cling so tightly that He can't take our self-life. Or we can offer our lives in the open palms of our hands and say, "Lord, here I am. Take what You want." When we yield all to the Lord, there is no stress or struggle when He removes or adds what needs to be changed in our lives.

We often initially perceive change as loss, but in the Spirit can we see a worldly loss as a gain. We can say, "God, if there is anything in my life that doesn't suit You perfectly, take it away and give me what does suit You perfectly." Of course, to do this, we must subordinate our will and our desires, because they are self-centered. We can have an active will and a strong desire if they are God-centered. We will offer no resistance when God takes away something we consider good because we know that He will give us something better.

The Lord once told my wife and me that we were to turn the leadership of a meeting over to someone else. Leading this meeting was part of our sphere of ministry, and we had fellowshipped with these people for some time. Yet the Lord said He had raised up another to take our place. "Release this meeting to him," He told us. If we had tried to cling to—own and control—this meeting after God had told us to let it go, chaos, disorder and confusion would have resulted because our self-life would have been ruling. God gave us the assignment. It wasn't our ministry. It was His, and we were to serve in it for a time.

We felt a godly sorrow because we had come to love those people with a whole heart. We were a part of them, and they were a part of us. Yet we knew that when God said it was time to move on, it was time to move on. We had not broken fellowship with them; we were still joined to them in the Spirit. We lost only from the viewpoint of our selfish desires. Actually, we gained—the Lord told us to work with another group. Giving up one and picking up the other was not stressful.

When God says to give up some of our associations, we often have trouble letting go because we think what we have is wonderful. We struggle and strain and hang on as God presses us to let go so that He can take us to something better.

I once had oversight of one group of a parachurch ministry. The Lord spoke to me that I was no longer to hold that position. At first I was troubled and thought I had done something wrong, but I had no conviction from the Holy Spirit. Finally, I yielded to the will of God and realized that I didn't *own* that position. Within days, I received a phone call from the person over me in the organization. He informed me that the Lord had instructed him to set me over five groups like the one I had released. If we hold the attitude that considers all change to be loss, it will frustrate the purposes of God.

As we overcome in the battles with the world and the flesh, it becomes easier to resist and defeat Satan and his demons.

> Hereafter I will not talk much with you: for the prince of this world cometh, and hath nothing in me.
>
> (John 14:30)

Wouldn't we like to be able to say that the prince of this world is coming but has no hold on us? Oh God, get us to that place! That is the place in which we will experience full freedom in every area of our lives. We will have all curses over us broken and be released from every harmful vow and every binding soul tie. The Devil will have no access, no doorway, and no sin through which to trouble us. We will be free. We will be dead to the rule of self, but we will be very much alive to the government of Jesus. We will not be out of this world. We will be in it, but not of it.

> I have written unto you, fathers, because ye have known him [that is] from the beginning. I have written unto you, young men, because ye are strong, and the word of God abideth in you, and ye have overcome the wicked one.
>
> (1 John 2:14)

Thayer's Lexicon says "strong" means "a strength of soul, to sustain the assaults of the enemy and remain standing." When the battle ends, we will be standing firm and unmoved (see Eph. 6:11-13). *Thayer's Lexicon* also states that the phrase "Word of God abides in us" means that it is "established permanently in our soul and always working, exerting its power and strength within us." "Abiding" means that it is not only there and remains but that it also has literally become a part of us. It is a source of strength within.

The Word says we have overcome the wicked one. Note the past tense. This is a positional truth because Jesus has overcome and we are in Jesus. We have overcome the wicked one now—not in the future or after death. Our conflict with Satan is to enforce the victory Jesus won and to take back what the enemy has stolen. Satan would love to have us stop fighting him and wait until we die to receive the blessings of God's kingdom. But that is not God's desire.

I used to pray for God to give me strength to endure trials, but God corrected me. Now I say, "Father, give me power to be victorious over this circumstance." I don't want to just endure trials; I want to get through them and come out the other side, having won the victory. To get from endurance to victory costs something. The self-centered part of us has to die to wrong attitudes.

> Ye are of God, little children, and have overcome them; because greater is he that is in you, than he that is in the world.
>
> (1 John 4:4)

Jesus is greater and infinitely more powerful than he that is in the world. Jesus has total victory. It is a monumental and majestic victory above everything and anything that Satan could ever do or hope to be. The key to victory is to know who we are in Jesus *and* to know who Jesus is in us. This must be settled in our hearts and minds. Then we will know that our enemy is defeated before the battle begins. In union with Jesus, we overcome Satan.

> Submit yourselves therefore to God. Resist the devil, and he
> will flee from you.
>
> (James 4:7)

If we are submitted to God and resist Satan, he *will* flee. Satan
is not free to do what he wants. He is subject to the Word of God
and has limitations and boundaries established by God. He is not
an enemy yet to be defeated. When Satan attacks, we must declare
God's written truth as Jesus did (see Matt. 4:1-10).

> And the LORD said unto Joshua, This day will I begin to mag-
> nify thee in the sight of all Israel, that they may know that,
> as I was with Moses, so I will be with thee. And thou shalt
> command the priests that bear the ark of the covenant, say-
> ing, When ye are come to the brink of the water of Jordan, ye
> shall stand still in Jordan.
>
> (Josh. 3:7-8)

> And as they that bare the ark were come unto Jordan, and the
> feet of the priests that bare the ark were dipped in the brim of
> the water, (for Jordan overfloweth all his banks all the time of
> harvest,) That the waters which came down from above stood
> and rose up upon an heap very far from the city Adam, that is
> beside Zaretan: and those that came down toward the sea of
> the plain, even the salt sea, failed, and were cut off: and the
> people passed over right against Jericho. And the priests that
> bare the ark of the covenant of the LORD stood firm on dry
> ground in the midst of Jordan, and all the Israelites passed
> over on dry ground, until all the people were passed clean
> over Jordan.
>
> (Josh. 3:15-17)

Military tacticians know that a river is a natural line of defense
because it is difficult to cross. Imagine the city of Jericho near a
river that has flooded. The defenders of Jericho believed that the
Israelites would not be able to cross that river. However, one day
from the top of the city wall, the defenders watched eight men
with a box on long poles carried over their shoulders walk into
the water. The water parted, and the defense line they relied on

was breached. Rahab reported that the inhabitants of Jericho lost heart at that moment. The battle was won before it began.

> And the LORD said unto Joshua, See, I have given into thine hand Jericho, and the king thereof, and the mighty men of valor. And ye shall compass the city, all ye men of war, and go round about the city once. Thus shalt thou do six days. And seven priests shall bear before the ark seven trumpets of rams' horns: and the seventh day ye shall compass the city seven times, and the priests shall blow with the trumpets. And it shall come to pass, that when they make a long blast with the ram's horn, and when ye hear the sound of the trumpet, all the people shall shout with a great shout; and the wall of the city shall fall down flat, and the people shall ascend up every man straight before him.
>
> (Josh. 6:2-5)

> So the people shouted when the priests blew with the trumpets: and it came to pass, when the people heard the sound of the trumpet, and the people shouted with a great shout, that the wall fell down flat, so that the people went up into the city, every man straight before him, and they took the city.
>
> (Josh. 6:20)

The Israelites simply obeyed God and won the victory through obedience. That is the way we are in God: He goes before us, and our enemies tremble at our presence. The Holy Spirit is moving, yet we are not doing anything.

The story of Gideon offers another example of how obedience to God brought a victory. Gideon faced an estimated 120,000 enemy soldiers. He gathered 30,000 men, but God wanted Gideon's army small so He would have full credit for victory. God told Gideon to send home (without condemnation) all those who were fearful, and 20,000 men left. Gideon had 10,000 remaining, but God still thought that was too many. He told Gideon that the Israelites might still take some credit if Gideon used 10,000 men to defeat 120,000. So God separated another 9,700 men and sent them home, leaving Gideon with only 300 men.

God did not send the 300 men into battle with swords and spears. Instead, they carried a torch in one hand covered by a pitcher to hide the light and a trumpet in the other. No one carried a weapon. When they surrounded the Midianite camp and suddenly revealed the lights and blew the trumpets, the enemy panicked and killed one another. Following God's instructions and fighting the battle His way resulted in total victory. Likewise, our victories come through obedience. God does not direct us by the precepts of our rational or logical thinking but by His wisdom.

> Be not be overcome of evil, but overcome evil with good.
>
> (Rom. 12:21)

> Not rendering evil for evil, or railing for railing, but contrariwise blessing; knowing that ye are thereunto called, that ye should inherit a blessing.
>
> (1 Pet. 3:9)

Retaliation is the world's way, but it is not God's way. "Vengeance is Mine" says the Lord (Romans 12:19).

> But I say unto you, Love your enemies, bless them that curse you, do good to them that hate you, and pray for them which despitefully use you, and persecute you; That ye may be the children of your Father which is in heaven: for he maketh his sun to rise on the evil and on the good, and sendeth rain on the just and on the unjust.
>
> (Matt. 5:44-45)

Loving your enemies is not the world's way, but it is God's way. We are to pray for those who persecute us. If we do it God's way, He will give us victory. This passage is among the most powerful spiritual warfare instructions given in the Word of God.

> The angel of the LORD encampeth round about them that fear him, and delivereth them.
>
> (Ps. 34:7)

I believe that the "angel of the Lord" signifies God's manifest presence. God provides protection when we are in right relationship with Him and have a right attitude about any situation in which we find ourselves.

> Now thanks [be] unto God which always causeth us to triumph in Christ, and maketh manifest the savor of his knowledge by us in every place.
>
> (2 Cor. 2:14)

God causes us to triumph *in Christ* through His initiative and power. He brings victory when we live in the righteousness of Jesus. We will have victory if we do it His way, in Christ, and with the right attitude.

> Hear, O Israel: The LORD our God is one LORD: And thou shalt love the LORD thy God with all thine heart, and with all thy soul, and with all thy might. And these words, which I command thee this day, shall be in thine heart: And thou shalt teach them diligently unto thy children, and shalt talk of them when thou sittest in thine house, and when thou walkest by the way, and when thou liest down, and when thou risest up. And thou shalt bind them for a sign upon thine hand, and they shall be as frontlets between thine eyes
>
> (Deut. 6:4-9)

As previously stated, the end of self-government brings us more into the nature of Jesus. We have complete victory in those areas in our lives that we yield fully to the government of Jesus because He is already victorious. Our victory is in Him. It is sensible then to say that knowing the Word—which is incarnate in Jesus (see John 1:1,14)—binding the Word to ourselves and applying it to our lives is another key to victory. This means the Word becomes part of us and we won't move unless it moves us, and then we move according to its direction.

> For the word of God [is] quick, and powerful, and sharper than any two-edged sword, piercing even to the dividing

asunder of soul and spirit, and of the joints and marrow, and [is] a discerner of the thoughts and intents of the heart.

(Heb. 4:12)

Occasionally when listening to the Word being preached, or perhaps listening to a song, the Spirit stirs us. The Word of God penetrates our being and causes a reaction, which lets us know that God is calling our attention to a problem within us or to an impending opportunity. That is the Sword of the Spirit touching something in our lives. When that happens, we should be wise enough to note what the Holy Spirit enlivened and make it an object of thought, prayer and meditation. God has raised an issue, and we must act on it by seeking the meaning and application of that word. This is the conviction of the Holy Spirit that is referred to in John 16:8.

Wherefore take unto you the whole armor of God, that ye may be able to withstand in the evil day, and having done all, to stand. Stand therefore, having your loins girt about with truth, and having on the breastplate of righteousness; And your feet shod with the preparation of the gospel of peace; Above all, taking the shield of faith, wherewith ye shall be able to quench all the fiery darts of the wicked.

(Eph. 6:13-17)

We put on God's armor, not ours. It fits, but it is His. We wear the helmet of *His* salvation, the girdle of *His* truth, the shoes of the gospel of *His* peace and the breastplate of *His* righteousness. We carry the shield of *His* faith (faithfulness) and the sword of *His* Spirit that is *His* word. I like to think this armor actually is the person of Jesus.

The night is far spent, the day is at hand: let us therefore cast off the works of darkness, and let us put on the armor of light.

(Rom. 13:12)

"Light" is called armor because darkness cannot prevail where there is light. Light in this sense means openness to the Lord and others and being true to the Lord and to one another. This is part of our protection. When we keep our faults buried within (in the dark), the enemy can access them. When we bring faults into the light, 90 percent of the battle is won. Satan can't touch what is in the light, but God can and will.

> This then is the message which we have heard of him and declare unto you, that God is light, and in Him is no darkness at all. If we say that we have fellowship with him, and walk in darkness, we lie, and do not the truth: But if we walk in the light, as he is in the light, we have fellowship one with another, and the blood of Jesus Christ his Son cleanseth us from all sin.
>
> (1 John 1:5-7)

Darkness has no power over light. This ties in with the idea of biblical separation. If we are in the light, we cannot be in the darkness, because they are mutually exclusive.

> Thou art my battle axe and weapons of war: for with thee will I break in pieces the nations, and with thee will I destroy kingdoms; And with thee will I break in pieces the horse and his rider; and with thee will I break in pieces the chariot and his rider; With thee also will I break in pieces man and woman; and with thee will I break in pieces old and young; and with thee will I break in pieces the young man and the maid; I will also break in pieces with thee the shepherd and his flock; and with thee will I break in pieces the husbandman and his yoke of oxen; and with thee will I break in pieces captains and rulers.
>
> (Jer. 51:20-23)

We are God's weapons of war. When He goes to war, we are His battle-axes. We can consider ourselves as weapons held in the right hand of God. He uses us to smite the works of the enemy. Many times, this smiting occurs when the Spirit stirs our hearts to pray against revealed wickedness.

My wife and I used to frequently travel along a particular road. Every time we rode by a small shop, I would be spiritually unsettled and feel that something was wrong. So each time I went by that shop, I would pray for the Lord to deal with whatever wickedness was there. This continued for three or four months.

One day as I was traveling that road with a brother in the Lord, we came to this area and felt that same oppression. The Lord told us to stop and go into that shop. When we did and looked around, we saw copies of a magazine that told people how *not* to smuggle cocaine (because they would be caught) and objects of perverse art. The place literally reeked of evil.

This brother and I realized what an evil place it was. So we went into an open space several feet from the proprietor, who was behind the counter, and called on God to look into that place to see what it was and what it was like. We called on the Lord to judge that place according to His righteousness in Jesus' name. Then we turned around and looked at the proprietor. He was wide-eyed, and his face was chalky white. We walked out without saying another word. Two weeks later, the place closed down and remained closed for seven years. Later, it was replaced by a legitimate business.

An X-rated drive-in movie theater used to be located on a road we traveled once or twice a week. Every time I would go by, I would pray, "God, judge it. God, don't hold back righteousness. God, look at this place and measure it, and if there be wickedness in the hearts and minds of the people, I pray for their repentance. But if they won't repent God, You judge." The movie theatre went out of business long before the advent of videotapes and DVDs.

We are God's battle-axes and His weapons of war. The authority of Spirit-initiated prayer from our mouths is the weapon. It is the Word that the Lord has grafted into us and spoken through us in righteousness. That makes it effective.

> Behold, I give unto you power (authority) to tread on ser-
> pents and scorpions, and over all the power (strength) of the
> enemy: and nothing shall by any means hurt you.
>
> (Luke 10:19)

"Behold" means to pay close attention. Jesus is calling on His Church to wake up and understand what it means to operate in His authority.

> For we wrestle not against flesh and blood, but against prin-
> cipalities, against powers, against the rulers of the darkness of
> this world, against spiritual wickedness in high [places].
>
> (Eph. 6:12)

The Church often has fought against flesh and blood. We may wrongly perceive people—even other believers who are different—to be our enemy. We have seldom applied our energies to fight our actual enemies. God has identified our enemies, and they are not flesh and blood. Our enemies are demonic powers in the satanic kingdom.

> For though we walk in the flesh, we do not war after the flesh:
> (For the weapons of our warfare [are] not carnal, but mighty
> through God to the pulling down of strong holds;) Casting
> down imaginations, and every high thing that exalteth itself
> against the knowledge of God and bringing into captivity
> every thought to the obedience of Christ; And having in a
> readiness to revenge all disobedience, when your obedience
> is fulfilled.
>
> (2 Cor. 10:3-6)

We wage spiritual warfare using spiritual weapons. The Greek word translated as "mighty" in this verse is *dunamis*, which means supernatural power. Our weapons are immensely powerful through God for the pulling down of strongholds that influence our mind, emotions, and behaviors. We are assigned and directed of God to carry out vengeance and punishment against demonic powers that He has judged. It is an honor to be able to go out at God's command to tear down the enemy, put our foot on his neck, and bring him under the feet of Jesus. That is our privilege! It is a glorious and majestic task delegated to us by King Jesus. While accomplishing this, we praise God and carry the two-edged sword that is the Word of God.

> Be sober, be vigilant; because your adversary the devil, as a roaring lion, walketh about, seeking whom he may devour: Whom resist steadfast in the faith, knowing that the same afflictions are accomplished in your brethren that are in the world.
>
> (1 Peter 5:8-9)

> If we confess our sins, he is faithful and just to forgive us our sins, and to cleanse us from all unrighteousness.
>
> (1 John 1:9)

For a long time, I thought that unrighteousness was the result of the confessed sin. Now I believe that unrighteousness is the *birthplace* of the sin. If we don't rid ourselves of the source, we will continue to sin in the same or a similar way. However, if we are attacked and are wise in how we respond, we will gain a victory. We can turn every demonic assault into a victory if we deal with it promptly and correctly.

> Thy word [is] a lamp to my feet, and a light unto my path.
>
> (Ps. 119:105)

If we do not live by the Word, we will walk in darkness and stumble because we have no lamp to light the way. We do not carry a lantern behind us but in front of us so that it will light the way. We must be led forth by the Word and by the Spirit, for then we will be victorious. Note that the Word is a lamp, not a searchlight. We will have enough light for the next step, but not enough to see the whole way.

A wise believer said that the worst divorce any church ever experienced was the divorce between the Word and the Spirit. Overemphasis on one or the other leads to a church being out of balance. Emphasis only on the Word will, through human intellect, lead to legalism. Emphasis only on spiritual experiences, without the balance of the Word, will lead to error and deception.

> Thy word have I hid up in my heart, that I might not sin against thee.
>
> (Ps. 119:11)

"Hid" means reserved, hoarded, or stored in abundance for the day of need. We store the Word in our hearts to keep us from sin that separates us from God (see Isa. 59:2). Our obedience to the Word brings a blessing and also prevents the enemy from gaining an advantage.

> The LORD shall cause thine enemies that rise up against thee to be smitten before thy face: they shall come out against thee one way and flee before thee seven ways.
>
> (Deut. 28:7)

This is a great promise. When the evil one attacks, he will encounter so much power and opposition that he will be defeated and flee in seven directions in total disarray. However, it is a conditional promise. Let us examine verses one and two of the same chapter.

> And it shall come to pass, if thou shalt hearken diligently unto the voice of the LORD thy God, *to observe and to do all his commandments* which I command thee this day, that the LORD thy God will set thee on high above all nations of the earth: And all these blessings shall come on thee, and overtake thee, if thou shalt hearken unto the voice of the LORD thy God.
>
> (Deut. 28:1-2, emphasis added)

If we want the enemy to flee, we must be obedient. We must hear the Word of the Lord and obey it. If we hear and obey, we will receive a blessing. When our enemy comes, he will be so utterly defeated that he will flee in confusion, and we will be victorious.

> And he shall deliver their kings into thine hand, and thou shalt destroy their name from under heaven: there shall be no man be able to stand before thee, until thou have destroyed them.
>
> (Deut. 7:24)

The Old Testament records the physical experiences of a physical people that are a shadow and type of the spiritual experiences of the spiritual people of the New Testament. The Old Testament refers to an enemy as a man or a nation, while the counterpart in the New Testament is demonic power or an array of demons. God says that not one of them will be able to stand against us. We will destroy them all. That is why Jesus said He has given us authority over all the power of the enemy. Nothing shall anywise harm us (see Luke 10:19). The victory is ours before we begin to fight. The only way we can lose is not to fight.

> And it shall come to pass [that] whosoever shall call on the name of the LORD shall be delivered: for in mount Zion and in Jerusalem shall be deliverance as the LORD hath said, and in the remnant whom the LORD shall call.
>
> (Joel 2:32)

"Delivered" means help and strength in wisdom and also includes being set free from the harassment of enemies. When we call on the name of the Lord, we operate in His strength, His power, and His authority, not our own. If we use only our own strength, power and authority, we gain nothing. We may end up like the seven sons of Sceva who tried to cast out a demon by calling upon "Jesus whom Paul preacheth" (Acts 19:13-16). Because they had no relationship with Jesus, they had no power and no authority. When they attempted to cast demons out of one man, he ripped the clothes off the seven men and drove them wounded out of his house. That is what can happen when we use only our strength.

> But now thus saith the LORD that created thee, O Jacob, and he that formed thee, O Israel, Fear not: for I have redeemed thee, I have called thee by thy name; thou art mine. When thou passest through the waters, I will be with thee; and through the rivers, they shall not overflow thee: when thou walkest through the fire, thou shalt not be burned; neither shall the flame kindle upon thee.
>
> (Isa. 43:1-2)

God tells us to fear not, because we belong to Him. He tells us that we will walk through the waters, not around them. He says that we will walk through the fire, but it won't burn us. Notice that He didn't say He would keep us out of the water and out of the fire—He just said these things will have no power over us and we will pass through them unharmed.

Many believers become upset when troubles come. They expect that being a Christian should be some euphoric life that makes them immune from difficulties. This is not true. God says whatever happens to the people of the world will also happen to us (see 1 Pet. 5:9). Our blessing and benefit is that God will help us through those difficulties. God promised to take the difficulties we experience and turn them into good (see Rom. 8:28). We are not exempt from trouble, but we have God who brings us through the trials and uses them as vehicles for change, transforming us into the likeness of Jesus (see Rom. 8:29).

> But in all things approving ourselves as the ministers of God, in much patience, in afflictions, in necessities, in distresses, In stripes, in imprisonments, in tumults, in labors, in watchings, in fastings; By pureness, by knowledge, by long suffering, by kindness, by the Holy Ghost, by love unfeigned, By the word of truth, by the power of God, by the armor of righteousness on the right hand and on the left, By honor and dishonor, by evil report and good report: as deceivers, and

yet true; As unknown, and yet well known; as dying, and, behold, we live; as chastened, and not killed; As sorrowful, yet always rejoicing; as poor, yet making many rich; as having nothing, and yet possessing all things.

(2 Cor. 6:3-10)

When many of us became Christians, we did not realize that we would experience the difficulties Paul describes in this passage. Because of this, when we experience an unexpected trial, we immediately question God and ask, "Why me?" Consider the sufferings of Jesus. When we suffer as He did, then we have something to talk about! Until then, this light affliction is but for a moment (see 2 Cor. 4:16-17).

Once when I was murmuring, grumbling, and complaining in my heart about all my hardships, I guess that God, who hears what is in our hearts, got tired of listening to my negativism. He said to me in a strong way, "Hold out your hands in front of you and look closely at them. Where are the nail holes?" Needless to say, I experienced quite an attitude adjustment that day.

Fight the good fight of faith, lay hold on eternal life, whereunto thou art also called, and hast professed a good profession before many witnesses. I give thee charge in the sight of God, who quickeneth all things, and before Christ Jesus, who before Pontius Pilate witnessed a good confession; That thou keep this commandment without spot, unrebukeable, until the appearing of our Lord Jesus Christ.

(1 Tim. 6:12-14)

We are to push on in spite of difficulties. The Word doesn't tell us to be a spectator; it tells us to be a participant. We are to run the race with patience and finish the course that God has laid out for us. Halfway measures won't do—we are not to start and then quit the race (see 2 Tim. 4:7-8).

Brethren, I count not myself to have apprehended: but this one thing I do, forgetting those things which are behind, and reaching forth unto those things which are before, I press

toward the mark for the prize of the high calling of God in
Christ Jesus.

(Phil. 3:13-14)

The operative word in achieving victory is perseverance.
This leads to perfection, which includes the concepts of maturity,
completeness and wholeness.

Chapter 11

PERFECTION

Do you believe that we can be perfected in this life? If you don't, why not? If you do, are you fully and energetically pursuing that goal? If you are not, why not? Perhaps we have a hidden place of excuse within us.

Herein is our love made perfect, that we may have boldness in the day of judgment: *because as he is, so are we in this world.*
(1 John 4:17, emphasis added)

Too many believers fall short of maturity because they believe they cannot be perfect until they are in heaven with Jesus. This wrong belief prevents these saints from striving for perfection in this life. Every success we have in denying self brings us closer to perfection. The more of our carnal nature that we conquer, the more we will manifest the perfection (character) of the Lord.

The disciple is not above his master: but every one that is perfect shall be as his master.
(Luke 6:40)

The word "as" means to be exactly the same, to the same degree, and to act in the same manner. A disciple must be transformed to become exactly like his Master in word, thought, and deed. Each time we respond to an individual or situation the same way Jesus did, we manifest His nature. We must compare our character to the character of Jesus to know how much perfection we have achieved.

> For who hath known the mind of the Lord, that he may instruct him? But we have the mind of Christ.
>
> (1 Cor. 2:16)

"Mind" is from the Greek *nous*. This is the ability to discern and understand the spiritual realm. Jesus sent the Holy Spirit to give us this ability. It is not rational reasoning from a religiously informed intellect (soul), but discerning by divine inspiration (spiritual revelation).

> *Let this mind be in you,* which was also in Christ Jesus: Who, being in the form of God, thought it not robbery to be equal with God: But made himself of no reputation, and took upon him the form of a servant, and was made in the likeness of men: And being found in fashion as a man, he humbled himself, and became obedient unto death, even the death of the cross.
>
> (Phil. 2:5-8, emphasis added)

The word "be" in the first sentence is an imperative verb—a command or an urgent request of significant importance. "You" is singular and refers to individuals. "Mind" here is from the Greek *phroneo*. *Strong's Concordance* defines *phroneo* as sentiment, disposition and concern toward something. *Phroneo* describes a mental habit or thought made evident by deeds. Motivation and attitude are more familiar terms, and are major components of character, along with integrity. These flow from our inner nature.

Jesus *humbled Himself*. He was willing to accept the Father's plan, to take the low place and to perform the low service. Jesus' deeds (actions) revealed His (*phroneo*) mind (attitude and motivation). He made Himself *of no reputation*. He was interested in the praise of God, not man, and didn't want to be an earthly king. He did not reject sinful, hurting people. He *became a servant*. He did not follow His own will, and He did not do as He pleased.

He spoke what the Father gave Him to speak and completed the work the Father gave Him. He was also *obedient unto death*. He revealed the nature of God the Father and did not compromise truth to avoid hardship. He accepted the ultimate of suffering and shame.

Webster's Revised Unabridged Dictionary defines "sentiment" as "a complex combination of feelings and opinions [acting] as a basis for judgments, decisions, or evaluations." It goes on to say, "A sentiment is an opinion often colored by emotion." What was the governing emotion that was evident in Jesus' actions? He let go of what was legitimately His as God to accept and embrace something much lower for the purpose of benefiting others.

What motivated Jesus to make such a huge sacrifice for us? I believe that it was compassion. Compassion is love in action. *Webster's Dictionary* says that it is sorrow for the suffering or trouble of another with the urge to help. "Disposition," according to *Webster's Dictionary*, is an inclination or a tendency, or one's nature or temperament. Jesus has the identical nature of God the Father. God is love. Jesus is Love personified!

Webster's Dictionary says that the word "concern" has a Latin root. The literal meaning is to be separated by sifting in a sieve. Figuratively, the meaning is to work something through with another. Concern also implies interest or regard for a person or circumstance. Stated another way, when someone is truly concerned, they perceive themselves as having a relationship or a connection to the situation involving someone else to the degree that their actions make it evident that the situation is truly important to them.

Jesus was so concerned for us that He became intimately involved with us. In the midst of our pain, trouble and despair, He connected with us so He could help us and do what we could never do for ourselves. Jesus said that we would do the works that He did and even greater works as well (see John 14:12). Therefore, we must share His concern for others.

For every one that useth milk [is] unskillful in the word of righteousness: for he is a babe. But strong meat belongeth to them that are of full age, [even] those who by reason of use have their senses exercised to discern both good and evil.

(Heb. 5:13-14)

Therefore leaving the principles of the doctrine of Christ, let us go on unto perfection; not laying again the foundation of repentance from dead works, and of faith toward God, Of the doctrine of baptisms, and of laying on of hands, and of resurrection of the dead, and of eternal judgment. And this will we do, if God permit.

(Heb. 6:1-3, emphasis added)

The word "therefore" in Hebrews 6:1 refers to Hebrews 5:13. We must exercise our spiritual senses to obtain spiritual discernment. This will enable us to distinguish between good and evil. The writer of Hebrews calls us to perfection. The phrase "let us go on" means to press on energetically and expend significant energy in seeking perfection. We should not be satisfied with just the minimal basics of Christianity. God desires to produce the likeness of Jesus in us, and He wants us to press into His kingdom.

Be ye perfect *therefore* as your Heavenly Father is perfect.

(Matt. 5:48, emphasis added)

Here is another "therefore." Jesus concluded the Sermon on the Mount with a charge to be perfect, which means all of the attributes of life that He gave in the Sermon on the Mount are specific to being perfect, complete, and fulfilled. In other words, they are instructions for Christian living.

David Wilkerson wrote, "Perfection does not mean a sinless, flawless heart." Man judges by outward appearances, by what he sees, but God judges the heart, the unseen motives (see 1 Sam. 16:7). David was said to have a perfect heart toward God "in all the days of his life," yet he failed the Lord often. His life was marked forever by adultery and a notorious murder. The basic definition of perfection is completeness and maturity.

In the Hebrew and Greek, the definition includes uprightness, being without spot, without blemish, totally obedient. It means to finish what was started, a complete performance. Wesley called it "constant obedience." A perfect heart is a responsive heart. It quickly and totally answers the Lord's wooing, whisperings, and warnings. This heart says at all times, "Speak, Lord, for your servant heareth. Show me the path and I will walk in it."

> Let the words of my mouth, and the meditation of my heart, be acceptable in thy sight, O LORD, my strength, and my redeemer.
>
> (Ps. 19:14)

The word "meditation" in this verse is strongly connected to the phrase "words of my mouth." The literal meaning is that of a musical notation, the song or melody in our heart. Meditation refers figuratively to our plans, purposes, and desires—whatever makes us tick. This is our internal thought process that affects, for good or for evil our external expressions. It is very likely that this is the point Jesus was making when He said, "Out of the abundance of the heart the mouth speaketh" (Matt. 12:34-35).

If we want to know the reality of what is in our hearts, we only have to wait until something goes wrong and then listen to what comes out of our mouth. *If we have to bite our tongue, it is evidence that we have heart disease!*

> Observe the perfect, and see the upright, For the latter end of each [is] peace.
>
> (Ps. 37:37)

When we observe the people who walk in the ways of God, we find that they have an inward peace despite upsets. They go through life in tranquility, secure in the knowledge of who they are in God and who God is in them. They are noticeably different from worldly people.

> Mine eyes shall be upon the faithful of the land, that they may dwell with me: he that walketh in a perfect way, he shall serve me.
>
> (Ps. 101:6)

If we have the heart attitude to do what is righteous in God's sight, He will regard us with favor. God views with approval anyone who sincerely attempts to live His way.

The Bible makes many references to character (perfection). The perfect heart displays unity and solidarity with others to do the will of God (see 1 Chron. 12:38). A perfect heart exhibits itself in liberal and joyous giving to the work of the Lord (see 1 Chron. 29:9). The perfect heart has integrity, which is expressed in faithfulness and righteousness, and will consistently act in a manner that brings honor to the name of the Lord (see 2 Chron. 19:5-9). Anyone with a perfect heart is so sensitive to their heart condition that they will never claim perfection (see Job 9:20).

Jesus revealed the nature of God our Father and, by His actions, set the pattern for perfection. Consider how He obeyed the Father, treated other people and was not self-seeking (see Matt. 5:48). Perfection means we will not clutch or hoard material goods. Instead, we will unselfishly look for opportunities to serve those in need (see Matt. 19:21). Perfection means we will control our tongues. We will speak no corrupt (defiling, negative) communication because our hearts have been changed (see James 3:2 and Eph. 4:29-32). We will not be critical, faultfinding or judgmental of others.

> Brethren, I count not myself to have apprehended; but his one thing I do, forgetting those things which are behind, and reaching forth unto those things which are before, I press toward the high calling of God in Christ Jesus. Let us therefore, as many as be perfect, be thus minded: and if in any thing ye be otherwise minded, God shall reveal even this unto you.
>
> (Phil. 3: 13-15)

Paul knew he had not achieved perfection. He adds, "I press toward," which means energetic pursuit. Then he says, "As many as be perfect, be thus minded." Note that this is present tense, not future tense. If God requires it, it must be possible.

> My little children, of whom I travail in birth again until Christ
> be formed in you.
>
> (Gal. 4:19)

It is not proper to say, "Well, I just can't be like Christ now, so I'll wait until I get to heaven." That is not God's plan. *Vines Expository Dictionary* says, "The word 'formed' refers not to the external and transient but to the inward and real." This points to the necessity for a change in character so we will be morally conformed to Jesus.

In one sense, we will not be like Jesus until we are with Him in our glorified bodies. However, we can reproduce His character and nature to make our lives more like His. We can manifest the perfection (character) of the Lord only after achieving victory over the world, the flesh and the Devil. Our determination and persistence to deny self will enable us to gain this victory.

> And above all these things put on charity, which is the bond
> of perfectness.
>
> (Col. 3:14)

"Charity" in this verse means unconditional love. The "bond of perfectness" that joins us in perfect array, accord and completeness is love. Love is the bonding agent.

> Epaphras, who is one of you, a servant of Christ, saluteth
> you, always laboring fervently for you in prayers, that ye may
> stand perfect and complete in all the will of God.
>
> (Col. 4:12)

"Complete" as used in this passage means to be crammed full. It isn't a container filled with froth; it is a container filled with a solid substance that is pressed down and packed to the limit.

Note that Paul again writes in the present tense, which means that we *today* can stand perfect and complete in the will of God. Paul is not talking about some future event. He is talking about attaining the goal of Christlikeness while we are on earth.

> Now the God of Peace, that brought again from the dead our Lord Jesus, that great shepherd of the sheep, through the blood of the everlasting covenant, make you perfect in every good work to do his will, working in you that which is well-pleasing in his sight, through Jesus Christ; to who be glory for ever and ever. Amen.
>
> (Heb. 13:20-21)

Perfection includes bearing fruit in the kingdom of God. If a fruit tree is mature, we would expect it to bear fruit. In his book, *Houses That Change the World*, Wolfgang Simson writes that the true fruit of an apple tree is not an apple. It is another apple tree.

> My brethren, count it all joy when ye fall into divers temptations; Knowing this, that the trying of your faith worketh patience. But let patience have her perfect work, that ye may be perfect and entire, wanting nothing.
>
> (James 1:2-4)

"Patience" means cheerful endurance in spite of opposition, difficulty or adversity. "Entire" means to be complete in every part, perfectly sound and whole.

> Seest thou how faith wrought with his works, and by works was faith made perfect?"
>
> (James 2:22)

The phrase "by works" refers to works specifically assigned by the Holy Spirit, not works originating from our own personal ideas (see Eph. 2:10). Any Christian who is a hearer of the Word and not a doer will never attain perfection, because part of the perfecting of our faith is to do whatever God calls us to do (see James 1:22-24).

In James 3:2, the author tells us that no man can tame the tongue. Note he didn't say the tongue could never be tamed; he just said no *man* is able to tame the tongue. Only the Spirit of God can tame the tongue. This is self-control, which is a fruit of the Holy Spirit. When we reverse the words "self-control" to say "control of self," it gives an interesting insight to that particular fruit of the Holy Spirit. Part of perfection is self-control, especially as it relates to speech.

Anyone who is being perfected in God's love, which is receiving love from and giving love to God, is being obedient (see 1 John 2:5). So, obedience, self-control, and faith are part of perfection along with works. These are progressions beyond the basic doctrines of Christianity such as baptism, repentance, laying on of hands, resurrection from the dead, and all those foundational truths. We are expected to progress beyond foundational truths while not neglecting them (see Heb. 6:1-3)

> Wherefore seeing we also are compassed about with so great a cloud of witnesses, let us lay aside every weight, and the sin which doth so easily beset us, and let us run with patience the race that is set before us, looking unto Jesus the author and finisher of our faith; who for the joy that was set before him endured the cross, despising the shame, and is set down at the right hand of the throne of God.
>
> (Heb. 12:1-2)

The phrase "lay aside" means to cast off or put away. "Every weight" refers to burdens and hindrances. The *Phillips* translation says, "Let us strip off everything that hinders us." Anything in our lives that is hindering us from achieving maturity must go. No matter how good it might look—or how good it might have been—it must go.

"Beset" means to cling to or entangle. If our feet are entangled in rope, it is difficult to walk. "Looking unto Jesus," according to *Thayer's Lexicon*, means "to turn your eyes away from other things and to turn them intently on the Lord."

Jesus is described as "the author and finisher of our faith." The word "finisher" is translated in the *Amplified Bible* as "perfector." We cannot be perfected (completed) if we do not constantly focus on the Lord. If we are diverted into focusing on anything else, we will stumble and stray. Perfection includes ridding ourselves of anything that turns us aside from the narrow way.

Sin isn't the only thing that hinders our progress. Scripture says to lay aside every *weight* that hinders us, which includes the emotional hurts that we drag along from the past. So, we have both weights and sins that hinder us from advancing.

> For consider him that endured such contradiction of sinners against himself, lest ye be wearied and faith in your minds. Ye have not yet resisted unto blood, striving against sin.
>
> (Heb. 12: 3-4)

Thayer's Lexicon states that the word "consider" as used here means "to contemplate by weighing and comparing your own burdens with Jesus." We should not consider the troubles we encounter as so significant that they impede our upward journey to be like Christ. If we remain focused on the Lord, we will maintain perspective. We can determine not to be discouraged and say, "OK God, I will exercise faith and patience until I overcome anything that confronts me."

We are supposed to be positive and optimistic despite our troubling circumstances. This is recognition of the Lordship of Jesus over our lives. If we understand that He is Lord *over* our circumstances, our circumstances will not hinder spiritual progress. We have His promise that He will work *all things* for good according to His purpose—that is, our being conformed to the likeness of Jesus (see Rom. 8:28-29). Contrast this with how the Israelites in the wilderness murmured, grumbled, and complained every time something didn't go the way they thought it should:

If ye then be risen with Christ, seek those things which are above, where Christ sitteth on the right hand of God. Set your affection on things above, not on things on the earth.

(Col. 3:1-2)

Our heart's desire and focus should be on what is important to the Lord. We should not over-focus on our future in heaven but rather be attentive to what will further God's kingdom in the present. We should seek His purpose and His plan in the midst of every situation.

This attitude will help us to not get upset when we find ourselves in stressful or frustrating situations, such a being caught in a traffic jam. We can say, "God you are in charge. I don't have to worry about it. I don't have to fret and wonder. I can take the time to praise You, to pray for the people in the cars around me and to intercede for whatever is causing the traffic jam." We can fuss and fume because we might be late, or we can take advantage of the time for Kingdom purposes.

And that which fell among thorns are they, which when they have heard, go forth, and are choked with cares and riches and pleasures of this life, and bring no fruit to perfection.

(Luke 8:14)

The people in this parable bore no good fruit because they were busy doing everything except the work of the kingdom of God. Of course, this doesn't mean we shouldn't mow our lawn out of fear we might miss something spiritual. Doing right things at the right time is part of presenting a good witness to the community. However, if the Lord says to deal with His kingdom things today and mow the lawn tomorrow and we don't obey, our busyness will frustrate God's plan.

God might ask us to do ordinary tasks at a particular moment because He has a divine purpose that we don't perceive. Once, the Lord told me to go and pick the fruit off a small pear tree in our yard. Even though I did not understand His purpose, I obeyed.

This set in motion a series of events that led to the salvation of two older people who died a few months later.

It is not wrong (sin) to have fine possessions. There is nothing wrong with being well off or comfortable, but if this is our priority rather than God, we will fall far short of perfection. The love of money (sin) is the root of all evil (see 1 Tim. 6:10).

> Are ye so foolish? Having begun in the Spirit, are ye now made perfect by the flesh?
>
> (Gal. 3:3)

We have all turned to God in the midst of trouble. When God helped, we were joyful and thankful. Then we told God we could handle it from there on by ourselves, and we immediately fell into more trouble. We can't organize, direct, orchestrate, or structure our Christian walk alone. We can only submit it to God and follow Him. When we try to do it on our own, we are living in self, not in His kingdom.

> And the very God of peace sanctify you wholly; and I pray God your whole spirit, soul, and body be preserved blameless unto the coming of our Lord Jesus Christ. Faithful is he that calleth you, who will also do it.
>
> (1 Thess. 5:23-24)

"Wholly" means to the full or entire extent, or a finished work and a completed act. Perfection encompasses our spirits, our souls and our bodies. Note the order in which Paul presents this: spirit, soul, body. One does not necessarily wait for the other, but the perfecting certainly begins in our spirits. It is clear that we do not sanctify ourselves. God calls us, and God does the work. The verb "do" is a powerful word in the Greek. It means to provide all the force, energy and power necessary to accomplish a work.

In Romans 12:1-2, Paul says, "Be ye transformed." Transformed means a total change from one thing to another that bears little or no resemblance to the original. The caterpillar that transforms into a butterfly is an example of total transformation. The butterfly has no resemblance to the caterpillar.

The Greek word *metamorphosis*, which means transformed, is also translated as transfigured. When Jesus was transfigured, He was so changed that He bore little resemblance to the man the disciples knew (see Matt. 17:1-2). His transfiguration was so dramatic, so complete, and so incredible that they saw Him in a completely new way.

The word "renewed" also appears in Romans 12:1-2 and describes a replacement of what was with something that is totally new. It is not a repair job or a factory rebuilt.

> Therefore if any man be in Christ, he is a new creature: old things are passed away, behold, all things are become new.
>
> (2 Cor. 5:17)

All things become new. The word "new" in this verse is not the Greek *neo,* which means to be made to look like new by refurbishing or polishing, but *kainos,* which describes something that has never existed. It is completely new.

The phrase "passed away" means to perish or to cease to exist. This does not mean it disappears for a time and eventually shows up somewhere else, but that it has been permanently removed. "Passed away" and "become new" in this verse are best understood to mean passed away and still passing away and become new and still becoming new. The original Greek expresses the idea of an ongoing process that is both fully accomplished in provision and is still being accomplished in experience.

> Finally, brethren, farewell. Be perfect, be of good comfort, be of one mind, live in peace; and the God of love and peace shall be with you.
>
> (2 Cor. 13:11)

Thayer's Lexicon says the meaning here is "to make one what they ought to be, that which God has ordained us to become." It means that we fulfill God's plan for our lives. This will not happen unless we cooperate with Him. God has a purpose, a time, a place and an equipping that He has planned. If we cooperate with His will, we will be perfected in the sense of completeness.

> And we know that all things work together for good to them that love God, to them who are the called according to his purpose. For whom he did foreknow, *he also did predestinate to be conformed to the image of his Son,* that he might be the firstborn among many brethren.
>
> (Rom. 8:28-29, emphasis added)

> But the God of all grace, who hath called us unto his eternal glory by Christ Jesus, after that ye have suffered a while, make you perfect, stablish, strengthen, settle you.
>
> (1 Pet. 5:10)

A Christian teacher once said that what God does not accomplish through grace He will finish through fire. If Jesus is really Lord in our lives, He is Lord over everything in our lives. We can look at the difficulties with the attitude that He is God over all circumstances. We can pray, "Lord, show us what You are doing so we can cooperate."

> All scripture is given by inspiration of God, and is profitable for doctrine, for reproof, for correction, for instruction in righteousness; that the man of God may be perfect, thoroughly furnished unto all good works.
>
> (2 Tim. 3:16-17)

The phrase "inspiration of God" literally means "God-breathed." The Holy Spirit will reveal through the Word and with proper understanding all we need to know. We will have all we need to accomplish all God desires (see 2 Cor. 9:8)

> For the perfecting of the saints, for the work of the ministry, for the edifying of the body of Christ.
>
> (Eph. 4:12)

God's purpose is to equip us individually for the work that He has appointed to each of us.

A man once had a revelation from God while he watching a football game. He saw 22 men on the field in great need of rest and 22,000 people in the stands in great need of exercise. He saw that this is what was happening in the Church—the work is so concentrated on a few people that the bulk of the work isn't being done. The man realized that the Scriptures teach that *all the members* of the Body of Christ are to function as servants of the Lord.

If the Lord is allowed to fully operate as the head of His Church, He will divide the labor, assign the functions and distribute the grace, gifts and equipping so that all will be active and no one will be overly burdened (see Romans 12:4-8).

> Now I beseech you, brethren, by the name of our Lord Jesus Christ, that ye all speak the same thing, and that there be no divisions among you; but that ye be perfectly joined together in the same mind and in the same judgment.
>
> (1 Cor. 1:10)

When we are mature as believers, it unifies the Body of Christ. We recognize, honor and respect the contributions of others, especially when those contributions are different from our own.

> I in them, and thou in me, that they may be made perfect in one; and that the world may know that thou hast sent me, and hast loved them, as thou hast loved me.
>
> (John 17:23)

Jesus prayed that believers would be made perfect in one, meaning unified. Maturity in any segment of the Body of Christ can be gauged, regardless of size, by observing how united it is. I believe that a good definition of unity is that which automatically occurs when everybody agrees with what God is saying. We must individually hear and obey the Lord to attain our alignment under Jesus' functional headship. We must obey without question or argument. Jesus often said, "Let him who has (listening) ears hear what the Spirit is saying."

Jesus had fully developed gifts and fully developed fruit of the Holy Spirit. He was obedient to carry out the works that His Father assigned. We are being perfected in the fruit of the Spirit, in the gifts of the Spirit, and in the works of the Spirit. When we are complete (mature, perfected), we will be like Jesus. His attributes, character, nature attitude, motives, intents, purposes, and ways will be fully reproduced in us and expressed through us. The life of Jesus will be evident in our mortal lives in this time and in this world (see Gal. 2:20 and 1 John 4:17).

Spiritual completion or perfection requires that Christians be in a connected relationship with other believers. The Body of Christ is not an organization but a living organism. The Scripture never states that a mature Christian should be anything other than a part of the functioning Body of Christ. We must enter a perfected relationship in which we give to others what God has given to us and in which we receive from others what God has given to them.

The giving of everything and the receiving of everything God gives is the functional level of perfection and completion. We will never be complete without each other (see Eph. 4:13). We are supposed to function interactively with other Christians as "every joint supplies." We will not attain the status or the fullness of Jesus in any other way. No one of us has it all, but all of us together have it all. God intends that we each be dependent on the whole Body of Christ for nurture and fulfillment.

A pastor once said the attitude of independence is not independence but an attitude of rebellion. The rebellion is against the plan of God that we should mutually submit to and depend on one another. We are not to be independent or codependent. We are to be interdependent and looking to God for everything.

We should fully appreciate that Jesus is to be revealed to the world today, before His Second Coming, through His corporate body functioning and acting like Him and doing the works He did. Jesus said the world will know we are His disciples if we love one another (see John 13:35). People in the world need to see Christians loving one another and interacting selflessly. No power, no idea, and no other religion can produce people who love, care for one another, and share in the same selfless way. Nothing compares to Christianity. When the world sees that loving relationship expressed between believers, they will know that we are Jesus' disciples.

Being like Jesus, acting like Jesus and doing the works Jesus did (perfection, maturity, completeness) is not only possible but also prescribed and enjoined. Furthermore, God expects us to attain it in the here and now, together. The more we are perfected—possessing the character and nature of Jesus—the more we will be true bondservants of love as Jesus was.

Chapter 12

SERVANTHOOD

Are you just serving God by doing what you want to do? Or are you a servant of God, doing what your Master directs? In the first case, you retain control; in the second, God controls. There is a great difference between these two positions.

Jesus did not come to the earth to dominate but to serve. His objective was to fulfill the Father's plans and purposes. We are called to be like Jesus, so we must serve at the will and pleasure of God and at the time, place and manner of God's choosing as Jesus did. That is servanthood.

> But made himself of no reputation, and took upon him the form of a servant, and was made in the likeness of men.
>
> (Phil. 2:7)

Jesus chose to give up the glory and majesty of the godhead in heaven in order to be born as a man and assume the limitations of human existence. He didn't come as a ruler or a leader or as a great man of wealth or power. Instead, He came as the lowest servant. The Greek word is *doulos*, which means slave. *Thayer's Lexicon* defines *doulos* as "one who is in a permanent relation of servitude to another, his will altogether consumed in the will of the other." Jesus modeled servanthood to His disciples.

For whether [is] greater, he that sitteth at meat, or he that
serveth? [is] not he that sitteth at meat? but I am among you
as he that serveth.

(Luke 22:27)

So after he had washed their feet, and had taken his garments,
and was set down again, he said unto them, Know ye what
I have done to you? Ye call me Master and Lord: and ye say
well; for [so] I am. If I then, [your] Lord and Master, have
washed your feet; ye also ought to wash one another's feet.
For I have given you an example, that ye should do as I have
done to you. Verily, verily, I say unto you, The servant is not
greater than his lord; neither he that is sent greater that he
that sent him. If ye know these things, happy are ye if ye do
them.

(John 13:12-17)

Just having knowledge about servanthood is not sufficient;
we must put this knowledge into action. In Jesus' time, washing the feet of guests was the job of the lowliest servant in the
household. Jesus didn't stop at lowering Himself to be man or a
servant—He chose to become the lowliest of servants.

But Jesus called them [unto him], and said, Ye know that the
princes of the Gentiles exercise dominion over them, and
they that are great exercise authority upon them. But it shall
not be so among you: but whosoever will be great among you,
let him be your minister; And whosoever will be chief among
you, let him be your servant.

(Matt. 20:25-27)

The word "dominion" means harsh rule. Jesus said that is
not to be a Christian's way. He said whoever is great or the highest among us should minister or serve. Jesus continued to say
that whoever is "chief," meaning foremost or in the first place,
should be a (doulos) servant, which is someone who chooses
to be a bondservant. A slave may have been someone who was
a captive, a prisoner of war or even one who was born into
slavery. Doulos refers specifically to a person who, when offered

his freedom, chose to remain a bondservant. It is a person who willingly placed himself in that position.

We can choose to serve. We can see something that needs to be done in church and quietly do it. We can volunteer to wait on tables at a church supper or offer to wash the dishes. There is a significant difference between choosing to serve at our convenience temporarily and choosing to be a bondservant permanently. One is function, but the other is an identity. If we choose to function as a servant, we can stop any time we wish, but if we choose to be a bondservant, that choice is irrevocable.

> But he that is greatest among you shall be your servant.
>
> (Matt. 23:11)

The Greek word for "servant" in this verse is *diakonos*, which means one who waits on tables, sees to the needs of others or functions to benefit others. This is the concept of servant-leaders as modeled by Jesus. We should be helping everyone advance into his or her individual calling (see Eph. 4:11-12).

Being a bondservant requires true humility. God says if we humble ourselves, He will lift us up (see 1 Pet. 5:6). It is not proper to pray, "God, humble us" or "God, make us humble." A study on the word "humble" shows that when God says to be humble, He means we choose to humble ourselves. Francis Frangipane likes to say that God intends for us to be more humble than we intend to be.

> Even as the Son of man came not to be ministered unto, but to minister, and to give his life a ransom for many.
>
> (Matt. 20:28)

"To minister" means to serve. This meaning comes from the Greek word *diakonia*, which means to serve in a low position.

> As thou hast sent me into the world, even so have I also sent them into the world.
>
> (John 17:18)

The Father sent Jesus to this world as a servant. Jesus then tells us that He is sending us the same way that the Father sent Him. Problems occur when people minister with a motive other than to love and serve others. This is contrary to the example set by Jesus. As He is, we should be also, including our attitudes and motives (see Matt. 10:25).

> But the Lord said unto him, Go thy way; for he is a chosen vessel unto me, to bear my name before the Gentiles, and kings, and the children of Israel.
>
> (Acts 9:15)

God instructed Ananias to lay hands on Saul of Tarsus. Ananias objected because he feared he would get into trouble. He knew Saul had come to persecute the followers of Jesus. God told him to go anyway, because Saul (who became Paul) was a "chosen vessel." If Ananias had refused, he would have hindered God's plan for Saul.

God has a plan for each of us. We have been chosen. We have been called into the kingdom of God for such a time as this (see Esther 4:14). If we don't seek God's plan and purpose for our lives with diligence, we may miss it. This is a terrible thought—to be a Christian and miss the purpose of God—but unfortunately, it is possible. Is God's plan and purpose for us clear to us? Do we know our destiny? Are we walking in it?

> But when it pleased God, who separated me from my mother's womb, and called [me] by his grace, To reveal his Son in me, that I might preach him among the heathen; immediately I conferred not with flesh and blood.
>
> (Gal. 1:15-16)

Paul realized that God had placed a call on his life even before he was born. God had specifically selected him and called him to be and do something he had not planned. Paul had freedom of choice and could have said no. Likewise, we have free choice. We can say no to God.

> In whom also we have obtained an inheritance, being pre-
> destinated according to the purpose of him who worketh all
> things after the counsel of his own will: That we should be to
> the praise of his glory, who first trusted in Christ.
>
> (Eph. 1:11-12)

The word "predestinated" has often been misunderstood. Predestinated means to determine in advance or to preplan. This does not imply to render inflexible and indelible but simply to preplan according to the good pleasure of God's will. Predestinated doesn't mean God has already decided our fate and we have no choice in the matter. The predestination of God is that He has a plan for us, but He will never violate our will except in judgment. If we do not choose to follow God's leading, we will miss His plan. It is our decision, not God's (see Rom. 11:29).

God didn't say, "Enter My Kingdom and tell Me what you would like to do." He called us, and when we answered, He invited us into His kingdom to live under His rule. He then tells us to go and live our lives according to His plan. We can say yes or no, but as with all choices, there are consequences. Every choice is a test. Will we choose God's will and way or our own?

> And we know that all things work together for good to them
> that love God, to them who are the called according to his
> purpose.
>
> (Rom. 8:28)

We are those "who are called" according to God's purpose. We are not called to comfort and ease. If we love God, we will keep His commandments (see John 14:23). If we don't keep His commandments, little will work for our good. If we don't walk obediently in the counsel of the Almighty, we will walk in the counsel of our own will, which will bring trouble.

> Who hath saved [us], and called us with an holy calling, not
> according to our works, but according to his own purpose
> and grace, which was given us in Christ Jesus before the
> world began.
>
> (2 Tim. 1:9)

God's purpose for our lives was established before we were conceived (see Jer. 1:4-5). We must seek it, yield to it, and enter into it.

> For he that is called in the Lord, [being] a servant, is the Lord's freeman: likewise also he that is called, [being] free, is Christ's servant. Ye are bought with a price; be not ye the servants of men.
>
> (1 Cor. 7:22-23)

We are no longer our own, for Christ paid a price to redeem us. The phrase "bought with a price" derives from a Greek word used to describe the buying of slaves. We may live with the attitude that we can do whatever we want, whenever we want, and God will somehow wink at this and say it is OK. A self-centered and self-directed life produces spiritual shipwreck.

> But in a great house there are not only vessels of gold and of silver, but also of wood and of earth; and some to honor, and some to dishonor. If a man therefore purge himself from these, he shall be a vessel unto honor, sanctified, [and] meet for the master's use, and prepared unto every good work.
>
> (2 Tim. 2:20-21)

If we clean the inside of the vessel and not just the outside as the Pharisees did, we will be appropriate, suitable for the Master's use and equipped for every good work. We need much transformation before we become true bondservants.

> For it is God which worketh in you both to will and to do of [his] good pleasure.
>
> (Phil. 2:13)

We serve God's will, not our own. We do not seek our pleasure, but God's. God might call us to places and situations that could be unpleasant. We must always remember there is a big difference between a *good* idea and a *God* idea. God ideas are always good ideas, but our good ideas are not always as good as they first seem. Good ideas usually please us. God ideas always please God.

We often become frustrated when God doesn't do things our way, in our time, or with our expected results. However, He never promised He would—He just said He would meet our needs and help us in trials. Expectations based on our desires and not on God's revelation often lead to depression when our desires are not realized (see Proverbs 13:12).

> Having predestinated us unto the adoption of children by Jesus Christ to himself, according to the good pleasure of his will, To the praise of the glory of his grace, wherein he hath made us accepted in the beloved.
>
> (Eph. 1:5-6)

When we follow God's will, the glory and praise will be His. When we do what He asks, be what He wants us to be and go where He sends us, He is glorified in us.

> But now hath God set the members every one of them in the body, as it hath pleased him.
>
> (1 Cor. 12:18)

God sets us in the Body (universal Church, local church, gifts and functions) where it pleases Him, not necessarily where it pleases us. If we have not ascertained that the church we attend is where God has set us, we could be in the wrong place. The Word says God sets us as it pleases Him. So if we have set ourselves according to our pleasure, our comfort, our convenience, or our friends, we have probably misplaced ourselves. We need to make sure that we are where God wants us to be.

> Wherefore also we pray always for you, that our God would count you worthy of [this] calling, and fulfill all the good pleasure of [his] goodness, and the work of faith with power.
>
> (2 Thess. 1:11)

In the parable of the talents, the servants with five and two talents traded wisely, doubling their master's money. As a result, both received the same reward: a strong commendation from their master with the promise of promotion and honor. However, the servant who was given one talent and buried it was strongly rebuked for being unfaithful and unfruitful. The master took back what that servant had been given (see Matt. 25:19-23)

God gives us many opportunities to witness. He gives us opportunities to serve. He gives opportunities for us to humble ourselves and to glorify Him. He gives us possessions. He gives us time. He gave us new life. Everything we have should glorify God. However, this can only happen if we enter into His plan, so that everything that He gives us is put to work for His kingdom purposes.

Many Christians do not understand that secular employment is full-time ministry. They see secular employment as interfering with their religious service. They believe they serve God only when praying or praising the Lord or reading the Bible or doing good works. This is not true. If God didn't want them to be in that secular employment, He would move them.

Servanthood is based on position and motive. We are servants of the Most High God even when we are placed in a secular workplace. If we focus on our identity—Whose we are—instead of on our work function or what we do, we will understand that we are serving the Lord. We will function in His kingdom 24 hours a day, 7 days a week, no matter where we are or what we are doing. We are ambassadors for Jesus, representing Him and His kingdom at all times and in all places (see 2 Cor. 5:20). Rick Joyner says that many of God's best pastors are found in schools and businesses.

God sets us in the place He has ordained for us to serve. We witness where we are—such as the supermarket while shopping for food—and we serve wherever we go. God wants us to touch the lives of everyone with whom we interact. If we see ourselves as Christians only when we are attending a religious service, we are missing a major precept of Christianity. Our Christian identity springs from what God has done for us, not our religious works. Understanding this identity will lead to servanthood, if we make that choice.

> I can of mine own self do nothing: as I hear, I judge: and my judgment is just; because I seek not mine own will, but the will of the Father which hath sent me.
>
> (John 5:30)

"Judgment" as used in this verse means discernment. We must set aside bias or personal agenda so that we can view people and circumstances through God's perspective with the Holy Spirit's help. If we view people and situations only through our own senses, our evaluations will be more carnal than spiritual.

Most of us cannot say that we consistently seek God's will over our will, yet we should do that as a lifestyle. Jesus set the example and told us to follow it. He would never have asked us to do this if it were not possible.

> And ye shall seek [me], and find me, when ye shall search for me with all your heart.
>
> (Jer. 29:13)

We can be intimate with God only when we seek Him with our whole heart. Our hearts can be divided. We can say "God, I want Your will" but actually mean that we want His will only to a degree. We can set boundaries for God without realizing it. People answer an altar call and say, "Father, I'll follow You anywhere. I'll do anything You want me to do, but I don't want to go to a certain place." Or, they say, "I'll serve You anywhere, except in the inner city." Or, "I'll do anything You want me to do, God, except clean toilets." The mind submits to the will of God as a religious act, but the heart is saying, "Hold it! I'm not going that far."

This represents the difference between serving and being a servant. If we truly desire to be servants, the Lord can tell us to clean the toilets and we will rejoice in doing so as much as if He had said preach a sermon or heal a sick person.

> Call unto me, and I will answer thee, and show thee great and
> mighty things, which thou knowest not.
>
> (Jer. 33:3)

"Call" means to earnestly seek a personal meeting. It is as
if we are in a place with a person we love deeply. We can't see
them, but we know they are present, so we go around calling out
to them. Being in the same place isn't good enough—we want to
be face to face with our loved one.

The Lord promises to reveal things to us that we do not know.
One thing that we don't know is His detailed plan. He says if we
will seek Him earnestly, He will reveal that plan to us. His plan
is not so hidden that we cannot perceive it.

> I delight to do thy will, O my God: yea, thy law [is] within
> my heart.
>
> (Ps. 40:8)

"Delight" means to desire or to have pleasure in. Do we take
pleasure in everything that God asks of us? Only what is easy,
right? It is fun to lay hands on the sick and see them healed. It is
much less fun to support someone who is going through a messy
divorce. Deliverance ministry is unpleasant and something we
don't really want to do. So we set limits and serve our desires,
but God calls us to follow His plan without restriction.

> If any man will do his will, he shall know of the doctrine,
> [whether] it be of God, or whether I speak of myself.
>
> (John 7:17)

If we choose to do God's will, we will know His doctrine or instruction. In other words, if we desire and choose to do God's will,
He will make sure we know His will in every circumstance.

> Make you perfect in every good work to do his will, working
> in you that which is wellpleasing in his sight, through Jesus
> Christ; to whom [be] glory for ever and ever. Amen.
>
> (Heb. 13:21)

God's will is not necessarily our pleasure or our comfort. God's will sent Jesus to the cross and took Paul to Rome as a prisoner to be executed—but only after Paul had written much of the New Testament. Likewise, the will of God may take us to places we do not want to go and produce results that may not be pleasant for us. Yet we can be certain that our obedience will glorify God and that we will have treasures stored up in heaven. When we stand before God to receive our reward, He will say, "Well done thou good and faithful servant" (Matt. 25:21).

Remember, the master gave the same answer to the servant given the five talents who brought back ten and to the servant given two talents that brought four. They had used what the master gave them to the best of their abilities. The master didn't commend them because of what they produced but because of their heart attitude of faithful service.

Whether we have five gifts, two gifts, or one gift or whether we do great and wonderful things or little things that are hardly noticed by others, if we are doing perfectly the will of God, our reward will be as great as anyone else's.

> No servant can serve two masters: for either he will hate the one, and love the other; or else he will hold to the one, and despise the other. Ye cannot serve God and mammon.
>
> (Luke 16:13)

Jesus didn't say it is difficult to serve two masters—He said it is impossible. We often attempt to have one foot in each camp. We do what we think is enough to avoid God's judgment so we can follow our own agendas. We serve God in ways that are not spiritual service and do things in the name of the Lord that are not what He asked us to do. It takes discipline to lay down our desires and to keep our focus on God's plan for our lives.

> I beseech you therefore, brethren, by the mercies of God, that ye present your bodies a living sacrifice, holy, acceptable unto God, [which] is your reasonable service. And be not con- formed to this world: but be ye transformed by the renewing

of your mind, that ye may prove what [is] that good, and acceptable, and perfect, will of God.

(Rom. 12:1-2)

Let us take a closer look at this passage. We cannot fully or accurately know God's will until we become a living sacrifice. That is a prerequisite. Unless we lay down our lives, we cannot know the fullness of God's plan. Our desires cloud discernment of the revelation of God's will. We can overcome this by telling the Lord that we have decided to do whatever He asks before we know what He will ask—and then mean it and do it. This is a costly decision because it denies self.

With that solid foundation, we can say "Yes, Lord" when we know His will. We will not struggle, because we have made ourselves a living sacrifice. We are entirely His. He can ask us to do anything and we will do it because it was settled in our hearts that we would before He even asked it.

And now, Israel, what doth the LORD thy God require of thee, but to fear the LORD thy God, to walk in all his ways, and to love him, and to serve the LORD thy God *with all thy heart and with all thy soul.*

(Deut. 10:12, emphasis added)

We can't have divided interests and serve the Lord with all our heart. God wants to bring us to the place where our whole being is yielded to Him.

With good will doing service, as to the Lord, and not to men.

(Eph. 6:7)

This is an inclusive statement: No matter where we are or what we do, we must do all things as if we were doing them for Him personally. This requires a major change of attitude from self-centeredness to God-centeredness.

If any man serve me, let him follow me; and where I am, there
shall also my servant be: if any man serve me, him will [my]
Father honor.

(John 12:26)

"Follow" means to become like the One we are following,
not just to go where He goes. We cannot be self-governing if we
follow Jesus. We cannot arbitrarily and unilaterally decide where
we will go and what *we* will do.

But seek ye first the kingdom of God, and his righteousness;
and all these things shall be added unto you.

(Matt. 6:33)

Seeking God's kingdom means yielding to His government.
Seeking His righteousness means determining to do everything
His way. We must pose the critical question first and foremost
that asks, "Lord, what would You have me to do?" We truly follow
Jesus only when we are in full obedience to His will.

We then that are strong ought to bear the infirmities of the
weak, and not to please ourselves. Let every one of us please
[his] neighbor for [his] good to edification. For even Christ
pleased not himself; but, as it is written, The reproaches of
them that reproached thee fell on me.

(Rom. 15:1-3)

A woman who had been a believer for several years came to
my wife and me for prayer ministry. She said that something was
missing from her life, but she didn't know what it was. As we
sought the wisdom of the Lord, He revealed a role-playing answer.
Steps led up from the room we were in. I said that I would, acting in her place, ascend several steps symbolizing some degree
of maturity. She, in the role of a new believer, was to approach
the first step, stumble and fall.

Acting as the woman, I expressed three possible responses.
First, I rebuked her for not watching where she was going. If she
expected to please God, she would have to do better than to fall

over something so easy as the first step. The second response was to correct her and suggest that there must be something seriously wrong with her faith, or she would never have fallen. The third response was to go down the steps, bend over and help her to her feet without criticism. I then helped her climb the stairs. The woman dissolved into tears as the Lord convicted her of being self-centered and neglecting the needs of weaker believers.

Part of our call is that the strong should serve the weak. This is opposite from the world's way, where the weak are brought into bondage to serve the strong. Jesus said that is not His way. Those who are stronger must be as concerned about the needs of their weaker brothers and sisters as they are about their own.

> For I am a man under authority, having soldiers under me: and I say to this [man], Go, and he goeth; and to another, Come, and he cometh; and to my servant, Do this, and he doeth [it]. When Jesus heard [it], he marveled, and said to them that followed, Verily I say unto you, I have not found so great faith, no, not in Israel.
>
> (Matt. 8:9-10)

Servants are under authority. God has established spiritual authority in His kingdom for His purposes, His glory, and for the accomplishing of His will. If we refuse to submit to righteous spiritual authority, we will never advance to true servanthood.

> Verily, verily, I say unto thee, When thou wast young, thou girdedst thyself, and walkedst whither thou wouldest: but when thou shalt be old, thou shalt stretch forth thy hands, and another shall gird thee, and carry [thee] whither thou wouldest not.
>
> (John 21:18)

Jesus told Peter that his days of doing what he wanted to do had ended. Peter was maturing spiritually and becoming a different person. He would go to places and do things not of his choosing. Peter was a stubborn, self-determined, self-willed man until he experienced a major conversion. The new Peter sought the glory of God.

> For though I be free from all [men], yet have I made myself servant unto all, that I might gain the more.
>
> (1 Cor. 9:19)

Paul didn't say he had temporarily chosen to serve (activity). He said that he had, though his own free will, chosen to take the permanent position (identity) of a servant.

> And if the servant shall plainly say, I love my master, my wife, and my children; I will not go out free: Then his master shall bring him unto the judges; he shall also bring him to the door, or unto the door post; and his master shall bore his ear through with an awl; and he shall serve him for ever.
>
> (Ex. 21:5-6)

The servant had fulfilled his servitude but made a decision to forgo his freedom. The servant loved his master, so he voluntarily chose to remain in the household as a bondservant. As a sign of his covenant commitment, by his free will he stood at the doorpost of his master's house while an awl, a punch, was driven through his ear, making a hole as a sign that he had made an irrevocable decision. A permanent hole punched in the ear was the sign of voluntary and loving servanthood. That is the highest place for a Christian.

Someone once said, "We may try to say I love You [God], but Your motley crew is another matter. Can't I just love you, Lord, without being invaded by all these other people?" We cannot. In the words of Theresa of Avilla, "Do you know when people really become spiritual? It is when they become slaves of God and are branded with His sign, which is the sign of the Cross in token that they have given Him their freedom. Then He can sell them as slaves to the whole world as He Himself was sold. We may be initially repelled to be made slaves of some people we know. To be a slave of Jesus is another matter. What greater honor could there be?"

The highest place in the kingdom of God is the lowest place in the world's view. Jesus was the example. Jesus assumed the lowliest role in the eyes of the world.

> The disciple is not above his master: but everyone that is perfect shall be as his master.
>
> (Luke 6:40)

The little word translated "as" is powerful in the Greek. It means to be exactly the same as and to the same degree. "Perfect" means the fulfillment of completeness and maturity. It means we have come to the place that God intends—namely, we have become like Jesus. Having become like Him, we can then do the same works that He did. We will have achieved the maturity of sonship and servanthood in God's kingdom.

From the Kingdom perspective, *success* can be measured by how much we become like Jesus and *satisfaction* can be defined as that inner sense of well being that comes when we know that we have done the will of God.

EPILOGUE

The Word of God effectively produces change (growth) only to the degree of our willingness to hear and our determination to yield to it. Jesus taught that we were to ask and keep on asking, seek and keep on seeking, and knock and keep on knocking. He promised that when we did so we would receive, find, and have opened to us what we so diligently sought after (see Matt. 7:7-8). I believe this Scripture refers to our maturing to Christlikeness, not to material prosperity, power, or even to Kingdom authority. These other things are significant, but God's primary objective for each of us is "to be conformed to the image of his Son" (Rom. 8:29).

The command of Jesus to "seek ye first the kingdom of God and his righteousness" (Matt. 6.33) sets the direction and priority of our spiritual life. To seek His kingdom is to seek His rule, not just His guidance. To seek His righteousness is to learn to do things His way, for "the Lord is righteous in all his ways" (Ps. 145:17).

I had been saved for several years when I had a vision of a horse and wagon. My experience had included many instances when I had sought the Holy Spirit for guidance in various matters and He had given me that guidance. The vision began with a view of me sitting on the driver's seat of a small buckboard wagon that was being pulled by a single horse. I had the understanding that this symbolized the context and content of my life.

The setting was a gravel country road lined with pleasant shade trees. The weather was ideal with blue sky, white puffy clouds, moderate temperatures, and a light, cool breeze. As I drove the wagon down the road, which curved to the right, I saw the Lord Jesus ahead of me standing beside the road, watching me approach. When I recognized Him by the welling up of the Holy Spirit within, I was delighted and stopped the wagon next to Him. I invited Him to come and ride with me and to be a continuing part of my life. Jesus looked at me, smiled, loved me, climbed up, and sat next to me. It was an absolutely wonderful experience of the presence of the Lord. I was overjoyed that He was with me in such a close way.

We continued down that country road for a distance, and then the road curved to the left. In the distance, I could see that there was a fork in the road. I spoke to the Lord and said, "Jesus, there is a fork in the road up ahead. Please tell me whether You would have me go to the right or to the left." The Lord looked at me, loved me, smiled, and didn't say a word.

I was perplexed by the fact that He did not answer me. I wondered if I had spoken with too much familiarity, whether I had not honored Him properly, or whether I had spoken too soon. Yet He did not seem to be offended at my question; He just didn't answer it. I knew instinctively that He was not being rude.

We continued farther down the road and came closer to the fork. Again, I spoke to the Lord, this time attempting to honor Him more and to be less familiar. I said, "Lord Jesus, You are the most significant presence in my life, and I don't want to do anything apart from Your will. Please tell me whether You want me to go right or left at the fork."

Jesus looked at me, smiled, loved me, and didn't say a word. Now I was very troubled. What was going on? I didn't have a clue as to why the Lord would not answer my request for guidance as He had done so many times in the past. Again, there was no evidence of displeasure in the Lord. I puzzled about this as we drew closer and closer to the fork in the road.

When we came to the fork, I stopped the wagon. With a great deal of frustration, I said, "Lord, I'm sorry if I am out of line here, but I just don't know what is happening. Your guidance is very important to me, and I'm just not willing to risk going on without it. Please let me know what Your will is so I can do it."

The Lord looked at me, smiled, loved me, and didn't say a word. To say that I was beside myself would be an understatement. I had no understanding whatsoever of why He refused to answer me, and I could not see any purpose in this whole situation. Things were not working for me as they had in the past. Something had changed, and I didn't have a clue as to what that was.

As I continued to search for meaning to this perplexity, I wondered to myself, *What does Jesus want from me in this? What Is He expecting me to do?* Then I looked down at my hands and saw the reins. *That's what He is after!* I thought. So I took the reins and placed them in the hands of the Lord Jesus. He looked at me, smiled, loved me, and didn't say a word.

We went off down the road together, and to this day I do not know whether we went to the left or to the right. But do you know what? It doesn't matter. The message in this is fairly simple: The Holy Spirit guides, but the King *reigns*.

CPSIA information can be obtained at www.ICGtesting.com
Printed in the USA
BVOW072105090512

289845BV00001B/2/A